PRAYERS FOR THE PEW

Bryce "Pete" Robertson

Acknowledgements

This Book of Prayers is dedicated to Stonebridge United Methodist Church in McKinney, Texas, for being able to offer these prayers each Sunday for nine years beginning in 1990.

The people of Stonebridge Church were so encouraging and complimentary. It is a privilege for me to honor them through this book. What a gracious congregation they are, and what a joy it is for me to honor their request.

The purpose of this Book of Prayers is to provide a resource for clergy who find it difficult to prepare a sermon and other material to present to the congregation on a given Sunday. A Pastoral Prayer takes so much time and energy to think and prepare. Anyone is free to use in whole, or as starters for their own unique style and presentation.

Thanks to Chari Sowers, Lisa Dethloff, Kate Edwards, Barb Frans, Cathy Wilcox, Mary Jeanne Jensen, Barbara Murphy, Fallon Collene, DeAnn Hoover and Dave Robertson for typing these prayers for publication.

Thanks to Country Club Christian Church and Senior Pastor Glen Miles for permission of photo for cover of this book. The photo was taken by my daughter-in-law, Diane Robertson.

Contents

Introduction

On April 15, 2015, I received a telephone call from my son, David, who is on staff at the Church of the Resurrection West in Olathe, Kansas. He asked me to share with him how I began, and continued for nine years, to write the Pastoral Prayer presented every Sunday at the Stonebridge United Methodist Church in McKinney, Texas.

I really had not thought about this particular exercise for quite some time, how something so perfunctory became a sacred ritual. Years before, in my Annual Conference responsibility as Director of Church Development, I had been instrumental in purchasing property for a future congregation in McKinney, Texas. Having been the purchaser of the property, a conviction came upon me, that surely God could use me in the initial formation of a new congregation carrying the name of Stonebridge United Methodist Church, to serve the needs of western McKinney.

After consultation with the pastor of the newly formed congregation, it was agreed that whatever my gifts and experiences were, I would begin, more or less, as a consultant to a promising congregation. It was also understood that I would be volunteering my time and talents, rather than receiving compensation.

When I first went there, the fledgling congregation was meeting in a public school cafeteria with the necessary 'set-up' and 'take-down' required each Sunday. At first, my responsibility was limited and uncertain. Then we moved into a new sanctuary and educational building, complete with offices, Sunday school rooms, kitchen and spaces for fellowship.

With the opening of the new sanctuary, my participation was affirmed on a regular basis, part of which was being the liturgist in worship, which included offering the Pastoral Prayer.

At first, the Pastoral Prayer was simply an expected part of a morning worship service. But within a very short time the Pastoral Prayer took on a completely different meaning. I began to realize the prayer was more than mumbling a few words to fill the space allotted in the bulletin. The prayer became a live instrument in defining the needs of the congregation, and enabling the people to enter into the presence of God in a new and exciting way.

The people began to look forward to the prayer, and I began to put more work into the preparation. This was a time the power and presence of God filled my life in a powerful way. I became more inspired to write prayers that connected with the needs of the people. The more I prayed, the more effective were my prayers. The more effective my prayers, the greater the response of the people.

Thus what began as a routine function enabled me to go deeper into a prayer life that was spiritually saturated with godly thoughts and ideas.

The prayers in this book are organized into three sections. First, as this prayer ministry developed, I began to organize my prayers according to the Seasons of the Church Year. Basically they are:

- Advent (four Sundays before Christmas Day);
- Christmastide (the 12-day period between Christmas Day and the day before Epiphany, which falls on January 6).
- Epiphany (according to Orthodox tradition was the day the Wise Men visited the infant Jesus and offered up their gifts).
- Lent (the penitential season that runs from Ash Wednesday to Easter. Easter is the only day of the Christian Year that falls on different dates. According to ancient tradition, Easter

always falls on the first Sunday after the first full moon or Vernal Equinox.)

- Eastertide (runs the day after Easter until the Day of Pentecost).
- Pentecost (the birth of the church with the coming of the Holy Spirit. Pentecost comes 50 days after Easter. Many churches continue to celebrate Pentecost until Advent.)
- Kingdomtide (runs from Pentecost until Advent. Kingdomtide celebrates the worldwide spreading of the Gospel message until He comes again.

I found it is very appropriate to use the Christian Calendar. This method enables us to follow the life of Jesus from the prophecy of his coming, through his birth and ministry, up to his crucifixion and resurrection. Prayer enriches each season of the Christian Year through a particular focus on a given season. For me to use this method is to broaden the scope of prayer to include given events to be celebrated during that special season.

The use of the whole Christian Calendar has certainly broadened my perspective on the special events during each particular season. If the pastor or preacher uses the lectionary, which are given Biblical texts for each Sunday during the Christian year, everything works more smoothly and effectively.

The second section of prayers in the book focus around certain special days which link the Christian Calendar with the secular calendar. For example, Mother's Day or Father's Day, Memorial Day or Labor Day. In this section you will also find prayers around events in the life of the church like groundbreaking for a new facility or a church anniversary celebration. There are also prayers for times of war or natural disasters, politics or elections, seasons of the year, or groups such as scouting.

The third and last section of the book are what I call General Prayers. These prayers are thematic around how God works in the lives of individuals and the Church or faith community. These prayers are written to tell us something about the nature of God and people; how that relationship is often fractured, but how God is ready to restore and heal the relationship.

Most prayers end with prayers of supplication around needs I knew were relevant to the people who were participating in the prayers in worship on any given Sunday. Sometimes I knew of someone grieving the loss of a family member, a friend or a job. Sometimes I asked prayers for those who were ill or lonely or in emotional or spiritual pain.

I must confess my prayer life has not been as meaningful as it was when I was offering the Pastoral Prayer every Sunday. There was a particular focus which I miss and it makes regular prayer a little more difficult and irregular. That does not excuse me, so I must work harder, with a different focus, to make prayer as meaningful as possible.

It is my hope you find this book helpful to your church's prayer life as well as your individual prayer life. Don't read these prayers as simple text or as study material, but make these prayers your prayers. Pray using a sentence or a paragraph, then add your own ideas, thoughts and prayers to God. Just as this exercise taught me how to pray, use it to teach you how to pray. In so doing I believe you will encounter God in the process and the dialogue between you will be life-giving and meaningful.

Bryce "Pete" Robertson
July 2016

P.S.- At the end of some of the prayers you will see a note stating "Also available on audio". I have had produced two audio CD's of these prayers. If you are interested in purchasing these audio CD's, contact my son Dave Robertson at daverob27@gmail.com and he can make arrangements for purchase and shipping.

Section One

Prayers for the Christian Calendar

May We Choose the Road That Leads to You

Into the holiness and quietness of your presence, O God, we bring our noisy and restless lives. As we move from Thanksgiving to Advent, we realize it is grace upon grace. In the season of Thanksgiving we acknowledge the richness of your blessings. In this season of Advent we begin to anticipate your visitation to earth.

As we begin our journey toward Bethlehem we find ourselves rushing here and there hoping to find you amongst the signs and symbols of a season too commercial. Yet, somehow knowing that if we will be still and wait, you will find us.

We acknowledge, O God, that at the beginning of Advent, you've given us the freedom to choose one of many roads. We may choose a road that leads away from you. Or, we may choose a road that leads us to your presence. The freedom to choose requires a conscience choice. Christmas comes to us, not by chance, but by choice. Grant to us a clarity of vision and a bold courage to choose the right road. Visit us, even now, O God, in the quietness of this hour. May we be born into a better mind, a more willing spirit and a more worthy life.

During this season of waiting:

- Bring peace to our troubled hearts.
- Bring joy where sadness is experienced.
- Bring hope where despair has held us captive.
- Bring love where hatred has prevailed.

In this season of joy and hope, enable us to deal with the realities of our humanity where illness, grief and disappointment are daily burdens, may your healing and redemptive love be experienced. May each day be met with godly possibilities. May the substance of the Gospel message become the foundation of our existence.

(Also available on audio- "And a Little Child Shall Lead Them"- Track 1)

Your Word Addresses a Broken World

At this season of the year, O God, your voice echoes through the centuries, coming to us through your prophet Isaiah who wrote, "For to us a child is born. To us a son is given. And the government will be on his shoulders, and he will be called Wonderful Counselor, Mighty God, Everlasting Father, Prince of Peace."

We hear your word, O God, and we await your promise. We confess your Word addresses a world that is dark and cold. Your people are so divided by religion, race and culture that hatred and violence often dominates the scene. So many of your people live in poverty with bodies racked with disease while the rest of us live with abundance, unwilling to share indiscriminately and generously.

In many ways, O God, we are a people living in darkness, waiting for the brightness of your truth and the warmth of your love. Your Word addresses a Church that is too often insensitive and self-focused. Our vision is too limited and far too worldly. During this season we are often misled by the appeals of the secular rather than being influenced by the sacred.

Enable us to celebrate this festival without false ideas, but with hearts open to hear and respond to your message. We affirm that at your birth heaven and earth were reconciled. Let us look forward to the coming of that light, which is beyond all lights, signaling the dawning of your eternal brightness.

We remember, before you, O God, all those who are sick in body, disturbed in mind, or troubled in spirit, as well as those who lack the material means of survival. May this season usher in a new attitude of love, peace and generosity.

(Also available on audio- "And a Little Child Shall Lead Them"- Track 6)

Give Us the Spirit of Little Children

God of all seasons, we welcome your presence as we begin our journey toward Bethlehem. We're grateful, O God, for your promise delivered to us by your prophets of old, that a Savior would be born and would deliver us from our human predicament.

Although we've experienced the joys of Christmas many times, O God, enable us to experience this season of Advent as if it were for the very first time. Build within us a proper spirit of anticipation and a holy habit of preparation. Reveal something to us that will startle us out of our spirit of complacency. Our daily routines have become monotonous. Our faith has lost its glow. Our commitments have worn thin. Impart to us your divine energy that we might once again experience your true spirit of the season.

Reveal something to us that will awaken us to new challenges and possibilities. Our lives have grown stale. Our goals have become glossed over. Pessimism has bloodied our hearts and minds. Take us to the mountaintop of our imagination and enable us to see the things dreams are made of.

Give to all of us, O God, the spirit of little children as we wait for the coming of the greatest gift ever known: the gift of the manger child.

(Also available on audio- "And a Little Child Shall Lead Them"- Track 2)

Holy Waiting

O God, as we continue our journey through Advent, we're not sure of what direction we should travel. We need a signpost or two that will offer us a clear direction. Enable us once again to focus upon that star that guided the wise men to the place where the Christ child lay.

We confess that we have become so settled in our own little niche that we lose our sense of expectation of what you can do in our life. We confess that we cannot see the brightness of your leading because our eyes are focused on the tiny candle of our own self-righteous enlightenment.

We ask, O God, that you would move us out of our own personal comfort zones and guide us to that place where authentic life begins. Snuff out the candles of our own ignorance and conceit that our lives can be bathed in the knowledge and wisdom of the one who transforms our thinking and will guide us to the head waters where faith begins.

We spend so much of our time waiting endlessly and needlessly for things that never happen. May these next few weeks be a period of holy waiting. We know that your promises are sure, so let us wait with hope that you will once again intervene in the affairs of your people and will enable us to reclaim the promise that the Savior will be born. Help us to realize the Holy Child is coming whether we're ready or not. Prepare our hearts for his holy arrival.

Enable us, O God, to realize the most visionary things we do in life are not fueled by reason or logic but by intuition, imagination and heart-felt desire. Keep the star before us this entire season that we too may be led to that place where the Christ child was born.

(Also available on audio- "And a Little Child Shall Lead Them"- Track 3)

May We Hear Your Call in Times of Silence

God of all seasons, yet who choose this season to verify the words of the ancient prophet that out of the stump of Jesse the Messiah will be born.

We confess, O God, that in the scheme of life, we keep looking to ourselves for answers that never come and for solutions to problems we will never discover. We confess, O God, we live in a culture that prides itself on staying busy. We surround ourselves with noise to block out the silence. A commercial Christmas comes with bells and whistles, the sounds of cash registers and the jingle of money.

The voices of our culture are many and exceedingly strong. Being still and quiet are not our way. Teach us in silence there is reverent intimacy. In silence we're able to hear your voice, clear and compelling, calling us to ultimate loyalty.

- We need to hear your voice of truth that denies all falsehood.
- We need to hear your call to righteous living that shuns evil in word or deed.
- We need to hear the soft cries of the infant child who reveals to us that love is the only way to a full and satisfying life.

Teach us that Christmas cannot be bought or captured by us. But the spirit of Christmas will capture us if we will but yield ourselves up at the manger in Bethlehem.

(Also available on audio- "And a Little Child Shall Lead Them"- Track 4)

Speak to Us, O God

Eternal God, into the peacefulness of your presence we bring our restless lives. We confess that we are tossed to and fro by the many winds that influences our lives. May we this day feel only the wind of the Holy Spirit as it seeks to unite us with all creation.

Speak to us inwardly. May your voice give us a clear direction and an unmistakable goal.

Speak to us through memory. As we hear the reading of your word and as we hear the music of the ages, enable us to realize that we are experiencing your mighty acts in history that speak of love and mercy On this first Sunday in Advent, stir our hearts with a fresh and convincing word that Christ has come and will come and is present with us as we wait for the final consummation of history.

Speak to us of hopes and dreams! As we tune our hearts to the messages of Scripture. As we sing the songs of the season. As we visually gaze upon sign and symbol, may our hearts be quickened and our hopes enlivened as we sense that our dreams will surely be played out in the drama of the manger at Bethlehem Speak to our wills! We are grateful, O God, that you have given us the power and ability to make certain decisions. We pray that we can choose between the high road and the low.

May the freedom that we exercise lead us into a spiritual fellowship that knows no boundaries and offers us the joy that we seek, but rarely experience.

As we travel the road to Bethlehem, may we have a singular focus and a determined will.

(Also available on audio- "And a Little Child Shall Lead Them"- Track 17)

A Savior to Lift Us Out of Our Predicament

We begin this day, O God, on that long and arduous journey toward the city where Jesus was born. Even in our day it will be a tiring journey, over rocky roads, unforeseen circumstances, and dangers.

Remind us, O God, that the journey toward Bethlehem is a journey of the mind, as well as a journey of the heart. Help us to realize that it is a journey toward hope, and a journey to a place where beginning again is a reality.

The journey seems monotonous, and we are often reluctant, not because it is so difficult, but because we are so unwilling. We feel ourselves to be pushed by tradition and social pressure, to make a journey we would like, very much, not to take.

Your sacred word proclaims: "that when the time had fully come, You sent forth your son!" The world of that day was ripe for rescuing.

But what about our time, O God? The conditions of humanity that existed then…still exists today.

- There are the poor who need to be taken care of and there are the rich who remain dissatisfied.
- There are those who are starved for knowledge and there are those who are academically arrogant and proud.
- There are those who wander from this thing to that and there are those who are seeking aggressive but often deceitful goals.

All of us, O God, are in great need of a Savior; One who can lift us out of our individual and selfish predicament. So let us wait with patience and hope for the answer to our needs is only a short distance away.

A Season of Hope

O God, your word reminds us that where there is no vision your people perish. You've also revealed to us that where there is no hope, your people are in great despair. We realize, O God, we are a people who have little hope, nothing to look forward to. And a people who no hope have no dreams or visions.

- A people with no hope live only in the present.
- A people with no hope are wandering in the sea of discontent.
- A people with no hope have no life purpose.
- And a people with no hope quickly lose their motivation.

This season of the year is the season of hope. Hope offers us the best things in the worst times. Our hope is not in humankind or material successes. Our hope is not found on the front pages of our daily newspaper or the breaking stories of our newscast. Our hope is not found in the skylines of our cities, but in the hills of our Lord.

We ask, O God, that you would give us a fresh confidence with which to face the future, knowing the future is in your hands. Take us to the manger once more and let us gaze upon the face of the infant Jesus, knowing that hope is born anew whenever we come into his presence.

(Also available on audio- "And a Little Child Shall Lead Them"- Track 7)

Our Hope Rests With the Promise of a Savior

O God, who strengthens the weak and lifts the fallen, we turn to you when our life is in shambles, because there is no one else to whom we can turn.

We confess that we are prone to walk in spiritual darkness. We seek the light of truth in most of life's endeavors, yet when it comes to matters of faith and spiritual discernment, we seem all too content to muddle our way through. We are bent on becoming successful in the superficial areas of life, and so deficient in the necessary ones.

We are ashamed of who we are and how our values tend to fluctuate and deteriorate.

There are some of us, O God, who are at the end of our rope. Our marriages are crumbling; we have lost the challenge in our work place; life has lost its purpose; and we are too often depressed and do not know how to overcome it. We seem to be running in circles, going nowhere, but becoming tired and discouraged.

We call upon You, O God, to lift us out of our lethargy, and awaken something positive within us. Surely there is an angel out there or a friend who can speak a word of encouragement, and offer us a glimpse of hope.

We sense that the secret that will bring us out of our predicament, has something to do with a tiny baby in an obscure part of the world.

Remind us that our hope rests with the promise that a Savior will be born, who will restore us to a right relationship with you, and will heal the breach between ourselves and our neighbors.

We have tried our way, O God, now give us the insight and will to live your way. May our lives become transformed and our actions become Christ-like.

(Also available on audio- "And a Little Child Shall Lead Them"- Track 12)

A Time of Waiting

O God, who willingly shares with us something of your divine nature, which possesses a love that is inexhaustible. In these moments, let us share with you some of our innermost thoughts.

It seems, O God, that we have been waiting most of our lives on one thing or another. Waiting is part of the human dilemma, and the reason for much anxiety and unhappiness. Our waiting is largely without hope.

- We wait to grow up and become independent.
- We wait to find our life-mate.
- We wait to have children, then we wait for them to grow up, finish school, get married and have children.
- We wait in line.
- We wait in traffic jams.
- We wait for that next promotion.
- We wait for retirement.

We know, O God, that waiting is often frustrating and unappealing. Waiting tests our patience and is often unfulfilling. We are a people motivated by action. We want to get things done, to accomplish something. We often wonder what we are waiting for, that we cannot make happen ourselves.

Yet, O God, you call us to wait. You remind us that our plan is not compatible with your plan. As your servant Paul wrote, "We see through a glass darkly", but you, O God, can see the total picture of how your Creation fits together. This call to wait is filled with promise and hope.

In this season of the year, you remind us that the message you spoke to the prophets long ago, is about to be fulfilled. Indeed Mary will conceive and bear a son, who will be the Savior of all humankind.

Let us not become entangled too deeply in the shaping of our future, lest we miss the signposts that will lead us into the presence of the only wise God our King who came in the form of an infant.

As we worship at the manger this special season, may we return to our homes and workplaces different persons because we have gazed upon the face of God in the form of an infant child.

(Also available on audio- "And a Little Child Shall Lead Them"- Track 19)

Grateful for Truth Revealed

Almighty God, whose truth is beyond our comprehension and whose love bridges every chasm, we gather as your people to praise your most Holy Name and seeking to understand the truths you readily reveal to us.

We are grateful for your truth revealed to us in the nature of this place we call the Universe!

- We are given the assurance that the planets move in their orbit, because you have so designed them.
- The sun rises and sets each day at your divine command.
- We are grateful for the seasons of the year;
    - For seedtime and harvest.
    - For the separation of the day and night.
    - For the warmth of the sun and refreshing rain.

The universe reflects your divine creativity and dependability. Although things are different, yet they are remarkably the same.

We are grateful for the truth discovered in every relationship.

- We know, O God, your divine relationship to us is intended to model the relationship we build with each other.
- The human family is but a microcosm of your divine family.
- The intimacies we share on the human level are but a taste of the intimacies you share with us on the divine level.

We are grateful, O God, for the truth revealed during this season.

- Grateful for the prophecy of our faithful fore-parents who gave expression to your promise of a Savior to come.

- Grateful for the reality of your incarnation in the Babe of Bethlehem.
- Grateful for the witness of your Son who showed us:
  - Love is stronger than hate.
  - Peace is better than conflict.
  - Mercy is the measure of your justice.
  - And commitment to a cause requires our highest loyalty.

Speak to the personal needs of each of us that we may experience the truth of your salvation born anew within our hearts.

(Also available on audio- "And a Little Child Shall Lead Them"- Track 5)

Come to us this Christmas

We welcome always, O God, the annual celebration of our Lord's birth. But many of our needs require your more constant presence.

Your coming, O God, has multiple meanings. Help us to grasp the greater meaning of your coming. You come to us in various ways and at various times – especially when we need you the most. So we ask:

- Come to us when our marriages become fragile, and are on the threshold of divorce.
- Come to us when there is disharmony in our homes – when parents and children are struggling over matters of authority and disobedience. Grant to all families a sense of divine cohesiveness.
- Come to us when there is instability in our work place – when our ability to maintain our life style is threatened.
- Come to us when we have difficulty maintaining fruitful relationships with neighbors and friends.
- Come to us when our attitudes turn sour, for whatever reason.
- Come to us when our bodies grow frail, and we can no longer perform the normal and desirable functions.
- Come to us to redefine the meaning of the season, when everything should be intact and joyful, yet it seems just the opposite.
- Come to us when we think that the giving of gifts is more important than the receiving of your most precious gift.

Make Christmas our reminder, O God, that you came, and that you will continue to come until the final consummation of your work.

God's Plans Are a Great Idea

O, God, we are a people blinded by our own littleness and short-sightedness. We need perspective, to see things as you see them. We need to see beyond the limits of today, to see what the possibilities of tomorrow are like. Our valleys are too deep. Set us on a high plain, so that we can see what is over the next hill.

We realize, O God that one of the most powerful things in the world is an idea whose time has come. Great ideas are rare and seldom come from us.

We affirm that Creation was a great idea, because you had a purpose in mind.

We affirm that the conception of Mary was a great idea, for it was a way you could become flesh and dwell among us.

We affirm that the birth of a Savior was a great idea, for it was a way for all humanity to be redeemed.

We affirm that everything you created should be ruled by moral order, was a great idea, for it is a way for all humanity to live together in perfect harmony.

Teach us to know, O God, that when Mary said "yes" to you, it was a great idea, and that it was an invitation to all of us, knowing that when we say "yes" to you, a great spiritual revolution begins in our life.

We affirm that the idea of the Kingdom of God was a great idea, because it bonds all humankind into one great family. The greatness of your Kingdom is experienced when gentleness prevails over aggression; humility over arrogance; simplicity over extravagance and love over hate.

Remind us, O God, that during this special season we are called to make your ideas a reality. Grant us the faith and strength to make real those ideas revealed through the birth, life and death of our Lord Jesus Christ.

(Also available on audio- "And a Little Child Shall Lead Them"- Track 8)

True Life Received as a Gift

Almighty God, teach us that true life is not found in acquiring or accumulating, but in the surrendering of ourselves to the One who has formed us. Teach us that life is not found in what we can take control of but by the One who takes control of us.

Help us to realize that surrender is not so much giving up, as it is the offering of ourselves as living sacrifices to the One who redeems us and will ultimately achieve His holy will. Surrender is not so much a matter of coercion, as it is a matter of self-will responding to the high calling of God Almighty.

We confess, O God, that some of us are selfish enough to think we are self-made persons. Some of us are simply drifting through life, allowing the winds and influences to carry us where they will. Some of us are shaped by the most uninformed, the most vocal, or by circumstances which have no scriptural basis.

Now is the time, O God, for us to realize that life doesn't revolve around us. Your scripture reminds us that we are simply the clay in the hands of the Master Potter, shaping us in His image.

Our journey toward authentic life begins at the manger in Bethlehem. May our focus be singular and intensive. Christmas is not for the taking, it is to be received as a gift. Let us approach the manger with open hearts, open minds and open hands, prepared to receive whatever the master chooses to give us. Let us live our life in the presence of the Holy One we worship.

(Also available on audio- "And a Little Child Shall Lead Them"- Track 9)

Finding Truth Through the Indwelling of Christ

O God, we know that life poses many great questions. We also know that answers are difficult to come by. You have taught us that truth is not handed to us quickly or easily. Truth must first be revealed before it can be discovered.

The answers to life's questions, do not come as an equation to be solved, but to be found as we form meaningful relationships with You and each other.

Jesus said, "I am the way, the truth, and the life". In order to discover the truth, it must come through the forming of a relationship with the divine mind and heart.

Help us to realize that truth comes to us through the alignment of heart and mind with the Master of the Universe. We may have filled our minds with an abundance of facts, but we will never know the truth without bonding ourselves with the Holy Child of all eternity.

We often experience life to be problematic and complex, which can become quite simple and fruitful when we allow the Christ Child to dwell within our hearts. If we can stay connected, that which He plants in our hearts will continue to grow until we enter your Kingdom as mature and responsible adults.

When our lives stay connected, we learn how to bring good out of bad; better out of good; and best out of better. The highest truth is not something we simply learn from books. The highest truth is a journey, a discovery, and an acceptance of your divine revelation.

May this season find us diligently searching for that truth, which is above every truth, discovered in a crude manger in the city of Bethlehem. To follow Christ is to live a truthful and godly existence.

(Also available on audio- "And a Little Child Shall Lead Them"- Track 10)

Holy Moments are Serendipitous

Almighty and everlasting God, we acknowledge that some of life's experiences are highly predictable, but some of life's greatest moments come with startling serendipities.

We confess, O God, that we plan, we connive, we work diligently to bring meaning into our own lives, yet rewarding spiritual moments often come as surprises from without.

We read the seasonal stories from Holy Scripture and the events surrounding the birth of the Christ child, but we realize that it requires the work of the Holy Spirit to offer us exciting breakthroughs.

The shepherds were simply on the mountainside tending their sheep, involved in their daily routine, when the songs of the angelic choir took them by total surprise.

The Roman government was simply taking care of business, when it received the shocking news that a King had been born.

The people under oppression saw little delight in the events of the day, yet a strange light glowed above the stable, and their hearts were suddenly filled with great joy.

Mary and Joseph were awaiting the birth of their son, but after his birth, were surprised by those who paid homage to their son.

It seems that no matter how much planning we do, our planning never quite measures up to God's surprises.

But what about us, O God? What about now? Will this season be filled with whatever we make it to be, or will you surprise us with some unexpected revelation?

- In our church, delver us from our stagnant routines, and surprise us with new revelations of your love and mercy.
- In our homes surprise us with some unexpected moments, where acts of love and kindness are generously shared.
- Give us a new attitude concerning our responsibility toward our neighbor.

May this season excel all other Advent and Christmas seasons, through a genuine encounter with the Holy One, whose name we cherish and worship, and whose name is above every name, Jesus Christ our Lord.

(Also available on audio- "And a Little Child Shall Lead Them"- Track 11)

Rooted in Faith

O God, Creator of all that is, we know that nature can teach us powerful lessons about life. We have learned that a plant has the best chance of surviving when its roots reach deep into the sources of water and nourishment.

We confess, O God, our lives are shallow and our roots lay too close to the surface. Because of that, our lives bear little fruit. In our shallow living, we make quick decisions, guided too often by intuition, or the whim of the moment. We are a people simply skimming the surface of what life has to offer.

Lord, we live the most of our lives at ground level. Teach us how to identify that part of us that can recognize and identify with you and your holy purposes. Help us to realize that it is the taproot that keeps us alive and in touch. Our taproot seeks to be in connection with your spirit, so that our lives can be fed with manna from heaven. The deeper the taproot, the stronger our faith. The stronger our faith, the better we can handle adversity.

Perhaps it is in this Season of Advent we will be born anew. Perhaps our life will be planted in spiritual soil for the first time. Perhaps something given birth long ago, will be renewed and quickened.

Prepare our hearts this season to meet the Christ Child in a new and accepting way. May we find a way to assimilate Him into our lives so that our roots get connected, and that our growth in spiritual grace will be experienced, not only by us, but also by those who seek Him. Let us not miss this great opportunity to set our lives on solid ground, and move in the direction of a Christ-centered life.

(Also available on audio- "And a Little Child Shall Lead Them"- Track 14)

Christ Will Continue to Come Until His Work is Complete

We welcome always, O God, the annual celebration of our Lord's birth, but many of our needs require a more constant presence. Your coming, O God, has multiple meanings. Help us to grasp the greater meaning of your coming. You come to us in various ways and at various times especially when we need you the most. So we ask:

- Come to us when our marriages become fragile, and are on the threshold of divorce.
- Come to us when there is a disharmony in our homes. When parents and children are struggling with issues of authority and disobedience. Grant to all families a sense of divine cohesiveness.
- Come to us when there is instability in our work place. When the ability to maintain our life style is growing more perilous.
- Come to us when we have difficulty maintaining fruitful relationships with neighbors and friends.
- Come to us when our attitudes turn sour for whatever reason.
- Come to us when our bodies grow frail, and we can no longer perform the normal and desirable functions.
- Come to us to redefine the meaning of the season, when everything should be intact and joyful, yet it seems just to reverse.
- Come to us when we think that giving gifts is more important than the receiving of your most precious gift.

Christmas is our reminder, O God, that you not only came, but that you will continue to come until the final consummation of your work.

Power Used Wisely for God

O God, in the creation of the universe, you established the laws of right and wrong. You have placed within us the ability to know the difference. You expect us to make decisions that will uphold your moral law and that we will take responsibility for our own spiritual development.

We confess, O God, that we struggle to do what is right, but we somehow find it beyond strength and will. Our hearts convince us what is right, but our minds often take issue with matters of the heart. Only your Spirit can teach us when to say "yes" and when to say "no".

We realize, O God, that power can be both good and bad. Power can be expressed in so many ways.

- Power may be experienced as an oppressive force.
- Power may be seen in the enslavement of people.
- Power may be experienced as office domination; marital disparity; parental abuse as well as childish rebellion.

Teach us, O God:

- Power can also transform.
- Power can judge and rule wisely and compassionately.
- Power can be expressed through unselfish love; through graceful consideration in competition.
- Power can support the forces of goodness wherever we find it.

Lord, enable us to recognize and resist the evil powers that seek to control us, and to trust the power that seeks to redeem and transform us into godly creatures.

O God, during this season enable us to know that the reason Jesus came was to give humanity a clear choice for good, and the power to makes those choices. Let us worship at the manger in Bethlehem as our acknowledgment of ultimate goodness and our decision to follow the Christ Child.

(Also available on audio- "And a Little Child Shall Lead Them"- Track 15)

The Power of Choice

O God, as children of your creation, you have given us the power of choice. The freedom of choice is both a blessing and a curse. It is a bittersweet experience that can lead us either to ultimate destruction or to the joy of human fulfillment. The curse comes through our desire to always please ourselves. The blessing comes when our insight, guided by your wisdom, leads us into right choices.

We realize, O God, that we are constantly confronted with many challenges and opportunities. We are called upon to make decisions in response to these challenges and opportunities. Given our basic tendencies, we are prone to follow our own appetites and whims. Herein, O God, lies the problem.

- There are the challenges of family responsibility. We must choose to invest or neglect. Enable us to make the wise and fruitful choice.
- There are challenges in our work place. Teach us how to be productive employers or employees. Turn our disgruntled ways into sweet tempers and kindly dispositions, with the desire to serve the greater good of all those with whom we work.
- There are challenges in our neighborhoods. Teach us how to be cooperative and neighborly. Prevent us from being a neighborhood nuisance or one who tries to dominate the decisions common to us all.

We know, O God that we are free to choose our own choices, but let us know that we are not free to choose the consequences of our choices. We are reminded by one of your servants that the greatest thing in the world is to will one thing.

As we contemplate on this Special Season, we ask you to help us shape our choices that are compatible to your will. May our focus be singular and our intentions pure. Let us look neither to the left nor to the right, but to keep our eyes centered on the One whose birth we celebrate this season.

(Also available on audio- "And a Little Child Shall Lead Them"- Track 16)

Bring Peace to a Complex World

O God, we live in such a complex world. We crave simplicity. Everything is growing more complicated. The economy is beyond our comprehension. The political process confuses us. Science is stretching the boundaries of our minds. We struggle to comprehend it all, but it is too much for our small minds to grasp.

World conflict worsens. The struggles of nations, races, cultures and religions baffle us. When we should be able to rally around some common ideas, we are poles apart on any given issue.

Technology is growing exponentially, much faster than our feeble minds can grasp, and much faster than we can develop the morals to address and guide the various issues. We seem to have stone-age minds in a high tech world.

- We long for simplicity; for things that we can understand and deal with appropriately.
- We long for a world where peace prevails; where neighbor loves neighbor, and where enemies become friends.
- We long for a time when churches would express a simple message of God's love; where vicious religious competition would revert to a loving and reconciling spirit.
- We long for a time when parent and child are in perfect harmony; where parental authority is based on pure love and where children are receptive, respectful and obedient.
- We long for a time when business practices would be based on Christian ethics; where employees are valued partners in the operation of every business enterprise.
- We long for a time when all decisions are based on truth, love, fairness and respect.
- We long for a star that will lead to that place where love dwells, in the form of an infant child.

May your disclosure be simple enough for us to understand, and clear and compelling enough for us to follow.

(Also available on audio- "And a Little Child Shall Lead Them"- Track 13)

Slow Down and Quiet Our Minds

O God, our human story is one filled with noise, conflict, loud conversation, and sounds of war. Even this season comes with a rush, a hustle and bustle that does not go away until after the Christmas event.

The shops are crowded and busy, taking on a commercial personality. The cash registers are ringing with a secular clarity. Everything is at a fever pitch.

We affirm, O God, that the divine story is just the opposite, it is one that is still and soft, quiet and reverent. We are noisy because the clatter tends to cover up what the quietness reveals. If we tell ourselves that if we just stay busy, our inner lives will not be exposed. Noise becomes a distraction from reality.

We struggle, O God, in the attempt to make Christmas happen. But Christmas is not something we do, it is something you do. We cannot bring Christmas about with endless activities, we can only wait for Christmas to come.

We know, O God, you rarely speak above the clamor of our daily activities, but rather you speak through a still small voice, that can only be heard in the quietness of the moment.

So we ask, O God, for you to still our hearts, quiet our minds and slow us down in our ceaseless activities. Direct our thoughts to your quiet message, heard only by those who are still and attentive. May we truly hear the divine story this season. Jesus was not born in the midst of chaos, but in the quietness of the stable. Let us be still and know that you are God.

(Also available on audio- "And a Little Child Shall Lead Them"- Track 20)

The Spirit of Advent is Peace

Eternal Spirit, who at creation hovered over the waters, and at your command, out of chaos came order. Surely the Spirit of Advent is the Spirit of Peace.

How contradictory, O God, is the world in which we live. People around the world are crying, "Peace, Peace", but there is no peace. In a world growing more chaotic every day, we long for that Word which turns our chaos into order, and our brokenness into wholeness.

We confess, O God, that many subscribe to the idea that peace comes out of conflict, and that the answer to violence is greater violence.

We claim to be a peace-loving people, yet our factories continue to crank out weapons of destruction. Teach us what it means to turn the other cheek; to walk the second mile; and to give our cloak as well. We have tried things our way, O God, enable us now to try things your way.

Let the Spirit of Peace and harmony prevail in the life of this congregation. Wherever there are differences, let us solve them with peaceful solutions.

You have taught us, O God, that family life should be a model of peacefulness, where husband and wife are true to their covenant, and where children feel insulated and secure. Show us how to satisfy our needs with something other than the acquisition of new toys, but with hearts that are spiritually focused on your eternal kingdom.

We rest entirely, O God, on your promise, that you will send someone who will bring peace out of discord. Assure us that Advent is a season of hope and peace, with our hope being, that at your coming, peace will prevail.

(Also available on audio- "And a Little Child Shall Lead Them"- Track 18)

Season of Hope, Peace, Love and Joy

Savior God, who comes to us from light years away, to share your presence with us in this Holy Season. You came as a child, but you brought us the greatest of all gifts, the gift of yourself in the infant Jesus.

- Caress us with your tiny hands.
- Embrace us with your tiny arms.
- Pierce our hearts with your soft, sweet cries.

Remind us, O God, that Christmas is indeed a Season of Hope!

The message of your prophets has come to pass when we are overwhelmed by our own sin and guilt, with no place to turn, you sent the Savior of the world, nestled in a crib in Bethlehem. Because of Him our darkness becomes light and our despair becomes hope. May hope become the anchor of our heart and soul.

Remind us, O God, that Christmas is indeed a Season of Peace!

We confess that our lives are cluttered and noisy. The ways of the world are too much for us. The media seems to focus on revolt and conflict. We hear the cries from road rage to battlefield. Remind us that at your birth, heaven and earth were reconciled.

Even though the winds and waves threaten our tiny vessels, we can dwell secure in that peace that passes all understanding.

Remind us, O God, that Christmas is indeed a Season of Love!

You gave us the intellect to share your truth. You gave us the wisdom to share your goodness. You gave us the free will to love that which is true and just. Out of your love we were created, and out of your love we have been rescued and redeemed. Teach us that in serving one another, we neither count the cost, nor seek reward, but think only of the common good.

Remind us, O God, that Christmas is indeed a Season of Joy!

Deliver us from our grumbling and doubts; from errors and mistakes; from stubbornness and defiance. Guide us by that star that stood over the place where He lay so that your infant Son might become our light, and that we may experience joy unspeakable.

(Also available on audio- "And a Little Child Shall Lead Them"- Track 22)

A Season of Hope, Joy and Peace

Eternal God, with humble footsteps and reverent hearts, we approach the manger at Bethlehem. Although we have made this journey many times, may our journey this season be the most meaningful and our experience the most unforgettable.

May this be, for us, a season of light! Remove from us the shadows of doubt, ignorance and prejudice. May your light enable us to search the darkest places of our heart, exposing those things that are corrupt, while enabling us to clear debris from heart and mind, and to overcome our fear of darkness.

May this be for us, a season of hope! Give us a fresh confidence with which to face each day. Enable us to affirm that the future is in your hands, so that we may know that all will be well, and all will be well.

May this be, for us, a season of joy! Remove from us all that makes us sad and remorseful. May our hearts tingle with excitement as we draw nearer to the Christ Child. Let us not speculate on what might have been, but celebrate what was, is and is to come.

May this be, for us, a season of peace! So many in our world are victims of conflict. Our own families experience, too often, the pain of brokenness. We need the peace of the Prince of Peace.

- May global conflicts come to an end.
- May the Israelis make friends of the Arabs.
- May every nation see itself under your divine rule.
- May the lion lie down with the lamb, and allow a little child to lead them.
- May those in military duty find safety in your security, and may they be reunited with their families in proper time.
- May the love that was born this season, be the measure of our love, one with the other.

(Also available on audio- "And a Little Child Shall Lead Them"- Track 21)

A Christmas Eve Prayer

Almighty God, who may be to us an often unseen but strongly felt presence – we lift our hearts in reverent praise.

May this short time in your presence bring to us a wealth of insight, a calmness of spirit and a certainty of faith that enables us to face each day with renewed confidence and to handle our difficulties with courage and strength.

As your gathered people this morning our hearts are beating with an intensity that signals we are about to experience again your invasion of the world in the form of an infant child. With humble footsteps and reverent hearts we approach this holy place. We realize that we cannot come to the manger without some awareness of why you came. So place for us a cross in the shadows of his crib to remind us of this unspeakable love.

- May we feel the brush of angels wings upon our spirits.
- May we hear the songs of an unseen choir.
- May we catch the glow of that light that overcomes the darkness.

We pray, O God, that you will cross the inner thresholds of our lives.

- That the Babe of Bethlehem will take up permanent residence in our hearts.
- That the drama of the gospel become imbedded in our hearts and minds.
- To the end we will joyfully proclaim that the hopes and fears of all the years are met in thee this night.

In the name of the One who was born that we may live triumphantly.

Christmastide

O God, we affirm the words of your poet:

"Love came down at Christmas, Love all lovely, love divine,
Love was born at Christmas, star and angels gave the sign"

We have had our annual pilgrimage to the manger at Bethlehem. We have, once more, witnessed the birth of your Son, who has not only had a powerful impact on our lives, he has also changed the course of human history.

Throughout this whole season of Advent and Christmas, in our more meditative moments:

- We have pondered the words of your ancient prophets.
- We have been inspired by the announcement to Mary.
- We have been impressed by the attentiveness of the shepherds
- We have been thrilled by the voices of the Angel Choir
- We have gazed upon the lowly stable, and
- We have heard the soft cries of the infant King.

We come this day, O God, with mixed emotions. Although the birth of our Savior was cause for great joy, we have sensed that somewhere behind the manger we saw the shadow of a cross.

From the beginning of Advent until now, it has been a long and arduous journey. We pray, O God, our journey will not end in Bethlehem.

The road ahead is long and difficult one. The daily grind is no cake-walk.

- May our difficulties be endured with a loving Spirit.
- May our monotonous tasks, find among them a few significant serendipities.
- And may we be true to our walk until we arrive at the foot of the cross.

Bless those who grieve for whatever reason, those who are ill, lonely or disenfranchised. May the spirit of the season lift them out of their particular distress, and join them with the fellowship of the faithful.

(Also available on audio- "And a Little Child Shall Lead Them"- Track 23)

Christmastide

O God, orchestrator of all seasons, we confess that we are living in the afterglow of Christmas. The star over Bethlehem burned brightly for a while, but with the passing of the season, we have returned to the routine as if it has never happened.

Perhaps there is a flicker of light at the place we saw the star, but the flicker is not compelling, and we know that we cannot live at the manger, life demands too much...

In our candor, we realize our many shortcomings.

- We live in turbulent times, caused too often by jealous nations seeking to broaden their own self-interest.
- Our hearts are far from being pure
- Much of our life is tending to the mundane
- We so easily become depressed when things do not go our way.

Help us to realize, O God, that there is but One way to live our life, and that is your way. We meet you at every intersection, with the freedom to follow you or to go our own way. When we follow our own desires our guidance systems fails and we always end up with negative situations.

We are here today, O God, because we have chosen to be here, for whatever reason. During this hour: Enable us to discover deeper layers of meaning and understanding. Reveal to us the abiding truth of your way. Call us to be Christ-like in all of our relationships and circumstances.

May we leave here this morning committed to those things which have the greatest spiritual values, and will reap the greatest spiritual rewards.

A Prayer for Ash Wednesday

O God, this day is the beginning of a new journey. A journey we do not necessarily look forward to because it is somewhat painful. But it is a journey that is essential for our spiritual progress. Lent seems to come too often, but it is necessary.

The ashes placed on our forehead are but a symbol of what is going on in the darkness of our heart. We have made this journey many times, but by the time the ashes wear off, we are back to our negligent lifestyle. It seems the more important things are celebrated for a moment, and then it is back to business as usual.

If we are to grow in our faith, we must take with great seriousness the High and Holy Days which help define who we are as Christ's Disciples. Our faith is contingent upon each one individually engaging spiritually in events that enliven our days and enhances our faith.

Ash Wednesday is both a celebration of the beginning of Lent, and a call to repentance. As we become contrite and meek, with a devout seriousness, our experience of this day can awaken us to a whole new opportunity to realize our shortcomings and lack of trust in your marvelous power to restore us to a more stable relationship.

May this day be but the beginning of a new life in Christ, where everything wrong will become right; and may it have a sustaining power that will carry us with devotion through all the days ahead.

A Lenten Prayer for Today and Tomorrow

O God, who loves us more than we love ourselves, we confess that we, too often, love ourselves more than we do you.

- Your love is offered unconditionally; our love sets limits because of selfish interests.
- Your love seeks our greatest good; our love is often motivated by what we have to gain.

May the experiences of this Lenten Season convict us of our own spiritual neglect and our inhumanity to each other. During this penitential season, O God, may our confession and your forgiveness be our highest priority and may our greatest desire be to seek to live in harmony with your divine will.

So in this act of humble contrition:

- Cleanse our hearts and purify our minds that we may be transformed into the likeness of our Lord and Christ.
- Set our feet on the right path.
- Guide our minds to think holy thoughts.
- Sensitize our hearts to the values of the Spirit.
- Strengthen our hands to do your work.

May this experience of worship be but a prelude to a rich and satisfying life in Christ, empowered by your Spirit, to be people set apart and holy, whose goal is always to please you and to serve each other with gladness.

We pray for all sorts of conditions of our weakened humanity:

- For all who are sick today and who may become sick tomorrow – we pray for healing and wholeness.

- For all who are facing tough decisions today, and for ones who may be facing even tougher decision tomorrow – we pray for wisdom, guidance, comfort and strength.

Be that abiding presence who offers release from today's problems and hope for tomorrow's unknown.

A Time of Reconciliation with God and Others

We give thanks to you, O God, for mercy that reaches out, and for patience that waits our coming back. We know that your love is ever ready to welcome us on our return. We praise you that through your Son you came to us with merciful forgiveness; and that your Spirit is constantly at work to woo us back into the fold with permanence.

We find ourselves once more in the season of Lent, which challenges us to a clearer introspection and a deeper commitment. It is strange that throughout the year we seem to move farther and farther away, but when we find ourselves in this season, we are encouraged to return, and once again experience the forgiveness that only you can give.

May each one of us have the courage to admit our vanities, our immaturities, and our conceits that keep us from following your will each hour of every day. Grant us such a sense of purpose that nibbling annoyances may not turn us from our calling.

In your love so demonstrated at the cross, break down all the barriers which separate us from each other, and claim the spiritual resources to build relationships that are everlasting. May we not feel the estrangement from any person, but discover a sense of true comradeship with our fellow neighbors, as well as those around the world.

In a world broken by struggles for power, may there be true reconciliation. For those suffering from sickness in any form, give them the assurance of a thorough and cleansing sense of true healing.

Now, grant to each of us a commitment to ministry that no task will be a burden, but become a delight; to love each other as you have loved us; and that harmony will prevail in this place the way you created it to be.

First Sunday in Lent

Almighty and Eternal God who dwells in high and holy places, yet in some mysterious way dwells within the heart of all of us.

We come, O God, in this season of Lent, aware of our need for forgiveness. Anxious over our failures and wrong decisions.

Give us the grace to look deeply inward.

- So minister to our inner lives that we may have the strength to rise above worrying temptations.
- To stand strong in the midst of unavoidable consequences.
- To keep faith and loyalty high, even when the world seems to close in upon us.

Give us the grace to look upward.

- May we seek the knowledge and presence of your Spirit so fervently.
- That we will experience the comfort of your presence so strongly.
- That we will know with absolute assurance that we will be able to overcome our weaknesses and fears with a victory of faith.

On this first Sunday in Lent, help us to recall the Lord Jesus in his days of temptations. May we turn to you as he did to worship only the Lord God who created us, sustains us and redeems us.

Above all else, O God, we seek the cleansing and purifications of our lives.

- Make us strong in a day we are tempted to be weak.
- Make us hopeful in a day we are tempted to be disheartened.
- Quicken our awareness of your presence and make us receptive to the urging of your Spirit.

Send Down Thy Presence, O God

O God, we affirm the words of the poet:

"Send down thy truth, O God, too long the shadows frown;
too long the darkened way we've trod;
thy truth O Lord send down."
"Send down the Spirit free, till wilderness and town;
One temple for they worship be; thy Spirit O send down."
"Send down thy love, thy life; our lesser lives to crown;
And cleanse them of their hate and strife;
thy living love send down."
"Send down thy Peace, O God; Earth's bitter voices drown;
In one deep ocean of accord; thy
peace, O God, send down."

In a day in which so much we desire is artificial – and so much we hear and believe is false – our prayer, O God, is that you will send your truth into our hearts and minds – that we may know without a doubt, what is true and genuine; what is lovely and good; what is decent and honorable. May we realize that truth is not what we discover, but what you reveal to us.

As we journey through Lent, may we be open to the witness of your Spirit with our spirit; may we be sensitive to the needs of those around us – knowing that you speak to us from above – but also you speak to us thru those around us.

May our Lenten journey be focused on the cross:

- May it be a time of cleansing and purification.
- May it be a time of honest introspection and deep commitment.
- May this church through its many ministries touch with love those who need to be touched.
- May its witness be clear and its challenge be convincing.

Bless those who have special requests. May your Spirit be a comforting presence to the ill and bereaved. May your spirit be a persistent and persuasive presence in the life of all of us as we seek to be your church in a troubled world.

Help Us Look Inward, Upward, and Outward

O God, during this season we are reminded how disordered our lives have become. We often compliment ourselves on how much spiritual progress we have made in our life. But, when we pause to consider how far we have come in true discipleship, we find ourselves embarrassed by our lack of progress.

Our failed condition is only the fault of our lack of faith and our limited engagement in spiritual activities. When we are truly honest with ourselves, we become ashamed of how little progress we have made.

So, during this period of Lent, let us resolve to make our dedication real and authentic.

Give us the grace to look deeply inward. We discover the current world is too much for us. No matter where we look, we see greed and prejudice, unfaithfulness and lack of intent to be revealing the true nature of our heart. Our hearts are not set on things above, but on the values of our society.

Give us the grace to look upward. We know where our values come from, but we are reluctant to make the sacrifices necessary, by devoting our time to meditation and prayer. Examples are all around us, but our eyes are closed to true disclosures of value and meaning.

Give us the grace to look outward. The needs of our neighbors are much stronger than our desire to provide for their needs. If our lives have been prosperous, shame us for our selfish blindness. We have attempted to worship with clean hearts, but it has not been reflected in the outflow of generosity.

Come close to each one of us, that we might find the dedication and caring to cleanse our own hearts through the outflow of our generosity. Out of weakness, let us find strength and faith out of fear. In the name of the one who was most generous and exceedingly gracious, Jesus Christ, our Lord.

Offering God Our Minds, Hands, Voices and Heart

O God, during this special season, we are reminded how we have forgotten the true meaning of Lent. Grant that we may reclaim all that has been forgotten or lost. This is one of the most important spiritual seasons of the Christian year, yet we forfeit it because our attention runs contrary to your will. So, may we offer ourselves as an offering to you.

Help us to offer our bodies to you, so we may live in purity and chastity all the remaining days of our lives.

Help us to offer our minds to you so that all of our thoughts may be pure and clean; so we may ever seek the truth, and never be satisfied with false propositions. May we think honestly, never evading the facts no matter how misleading they are.

Help us to offer our hands to you, that you may use them in whatever way you can to make life more fulfilling to others as well as to ourselves. Enable us to use our hands for serving humankind, to make their life better, and to make our life more rewarding.

Help us to use our voice as heralds of your grace; and through us bring comfort and courage to all whom we meet and touch.

Help us to give our hearts to you, so we may love you more and seek nothing but to please you; and to fear nothing but to grieve you.

During this season, help us to give back to you the life we owe, offering our total selves, mind, heart and spirit; that in your service we may find our freedom, our peace, and our dedication; that this season will always have special meaning, spiritual renewal, and empowering reward from this time now and forever more.

A Lenten Confession

O God, we praise and magnify thy holy name. One of the most important seasons of the Christian year is the season of Lent. Yet, it comes with unwelcome hearts, for Lent tends to expose who we really are.

In your presence this day, we confess, as we lay open our souls to a loving and forgiving God, we seem to be better than we really are. We keep telling ourselves how good and faithful we are, yet we betray you at every turn.

O God, we ask your forgiveness for every weak moment where we cave in to the world's temptations. It isn't that we do not know better. It is that we lose our will in the face of many temptations.

So we genuinely ask your most gracious forgiveness for every weak and defiling thought which our minds harbor. For every word uttered when silence was the better act. For every word spoken in hastiness or passion when we acted out of character.

We ask forgiveness:

- For every opportunity lost.
- For every blessing thanklessly received.
- For every stumbling block we have placed in someone else's path.
- For speaking ill against someone when praise would have been better.
- For criticizing others when silence would have been golden.
- For failure to help when service would have been better.

O God, bless all those near and dear to us. May we compliment their good deeds and refrain from criticizing them when we think they have not done what they should.

Grant, as the days go by, the Spirit will take charge of our hearts, giving us victory over all of our sinful ways.

May we learn, this season, what it means to truly forgive. May we put into practice the true Christian spirit in all of our relationships.

Rescue Us From Routine

O God, may this season of Lent be for us an opportunity for renewal, more so than a self-accusing commentary on our sinful condition. Free us from the negative habits that consume our time; and from the monotony of our daily existence.

O God, rescue us from the routine! We confess, in our homes, we wake and sleep; we eat and do our chores; we scold and occasionally laugh; and we are caught up in the same tired conversations. Where is the joy that comes from marriage and parenting? O God, rescue us from the routine!

We confess that in our work we sift through papers; we gaze at a computer screen; we sell another house; we peddle the same old products or services. We complete the merger; we review company policies looking for shortcuts to work days or early retirement. Where, O God, is the satisfaction that comes with accomplishment? Where is the excitement of offering something constructive or beneficial to our clients? O God, rescue us from the routine!

We confess, O God, in our play we engage in our games half-heartedly. We call it recreation, but to us it resembles work. How can our leisure moments be creative without being so costly? Where, O God, can we find our minds refreshed, our energies renewed, and our hopes reborn? O God, rescue us from the routine!

From this season, O God, teach us valuable lessons. Routine doesn't have to change if we do. Routine doesn't have to be boring if we bring a creative energy to it. Enable us to find excitement in the ordinary; and to find the sacred that is embedded in the crevices of our daily life.

Let us embrace today with a heartfelt gratitude and be prepared to receive tomorrow with joyful anticipation.

May Lent Be a Season of Tears

O God, as we begin our journey through Lent, let it be, for us, a season of tears. Tears are expressions of our deepest emotions—solemn but powerful—painful, yet cleansing.

In our more somber moments, O God, we realize there are issues of the heart that cause our emotions to well up inside us with their outlet being tears that flow freely.

As we lay our hearts bare before you, O God, we realize there are:

- Tears of remorse, strong feelings reflecting our spiritual disobedience.
- Tears of regret which comes from hurtful words and acts committed against you and each other.
- Tears of separation from broken relationships which need mending. Our tears will not go away until we are reconciled.
- Tears from our human losses, where lives are taken away and possessions lost from forces beyond our control.
- Tears over conflict, real or imagined. Grief over a splintered world where nation is against nation, religion against religion, and ideology against ideology.

O God, let no eye, in this place, be dry from spiritual complacency. May we be your covenant community where our tears are shed, not reluctantly, but unashamedly; where confession is offered in true humility; where forgiveness received as an act of pure grace; and where tears of joy accompany our restoration as children to a loving and gracious Father.

Help us to know, O God, there would be no rainbow for the soul if there were no tears.

Meet us this day at the deepest point of our need.

Give Us the Grace to Be Renewed in the Likeness of Christ

Eternal God, Creator of all that is good, Father of all humankind, we turn to you this Lenten Season confessing our sin and pleading for restitution. So much is wrong in our world, and so much is wrong in our lives. We have a strange fascination with false gods, and we continue to seek things that are contrary with your will. We feed the lusts of our bodies while our souls are starving for spiritual companionship.

Give us the grace, O God, to look inward! Walk through the corridors of our heart; penetrate the secret places of our soul that we shield from each other and from you. Deliver us from the torment of double mindedness and give us the courage to lay bare our souls, and the honesty to accept what we see and feel that is, in any way, ungodly.

Give us the grace to look upward! May our eyes be directed heavenward. May our ears hear your voice above all others. May our hands be raised in praise, and may our hearts beat in rhythm with your heart.

Give us the grace, O God, to look forward! Make us strong in a day when we are tempted to be weak. May we be hopeful in a day when we are tempted to be disheartened. Enable us to see the possibilities within each of us, and may we be found pressing on to your high calling in Christ Jesus.

Convince us, O God, a good world cannot be made out of evil and unrighteous people. Convince us our lives can be renewed in the likeness of Christ. Convince us a new and glorious day can be born out of the chaos and confusion of the world's disorder. Convince us from this time forward, we can be Christ to our neighbor, and the Church can become the true Body of Christ in a broken world.

The Road to the Cross

O God, as we journey through Lent, we realize there are many roads we may choose to follow, but there is only one road that leads us to the foot of the cross.

As we seek to choose the road upon which we will travel, may our choice be informed and inspired. Help us to know that to choose a road is to choose a lifestyle. To choose a road is to also choose its destination.

During this season, O God, enable us to choose to walk the road of spiritual discipline, where worship, prayer and fasting become holy habits which shape our life, and become a permanent part of our daily ritual.

Enable us, O God, to walk the road of personal sacrifice, where we are willing to give up those things which stunt our spiritual growth, and give up those things that create barriers between ourselves and you, as well as each other.

Enable us, O God, to walk the road to peace. We pray for our servicemen and women. May their journey become one which will ultimately bring about a new nation, not ruled by fear, but ruled by principles which recognize and affirm the worth and dignity of all persons.

Enable us, O God, in our daily living, to walk the road of moral and spiritual integrity, where word and deed are in perfect harmony.

Let us follow in the footsteps of the One who always made right choices, even as he set his face toward Jerusalem.

Be to us this day, O God, whatever our hearts long for, and whatever brings peace and contentment to our souls.

Forgive Us, Strengthen Us, Renew Us, Enable Us

Most merciful Father, who is always more ready to hear than we are to pray; and One who gives us more than we deserve or desire, pour down your grace upon us, forgiving us all those things our conscience convicts us.

Grant to us all the good things we are not worthy to ask, knowing you are far more forgiving than we can ever imagine. Lent provides us the opportunity to lay all our sins before you, knowing your mercy is greater than we can imagine or hope for.

We ask you go beyond our personal and daily needs, and minister to a world of unbridled passions and desires. We confess we are a broken and undeserving family filled with greed and selfish desires. The world is far beyond our abilities to minister to and heal. Only you can bring us together as one family.

Place upon us the responsibilities we can handle, and strengthen us to tolerate the ones we cannot. This calls for a total reliance upon you to manage the issues with which we fail. Expect and strengthen us to handle the issues within our capability with grace and commitment.

May each one of us bring a fresh and powerful commitment to become involved in the issues of our day, with a renewed spirit, endowed by your grace.

May this season awaken us to a new and fresh responsibility where we are in contact with your Spirit. Help us be willing to give our all to the advancement of Your Kingdom.

Refine Us Through Your Fire of Love

O God, who is from everlasting to everlasting, world without end. We would seek to understand our destiny on this planet, somewhere in space. We are so small and you are so great. Our planet is but a speck of cosmic dust compared to the Universe, and we are so insignificant in comparison to your being.

As we travel through the season of Lent, we acknowledge the gross and selfish thoughts we so harbor in our hearts and minds.

We confess we allow our thoughts to wander down unclean and forbidden ways. We often deceive ourselves by thinking we are on the right path when we are wandering in the wilderness, unable to comprehend the truth and unwilling to follow what we know to be the right way.

We pretend to be better than we are, and we deceive ourselves believing we have discovered the truth, when we have but touched a particle of what is real and true.

We know honesty and true confession is the better policy, but somehow we cannot know the truth from false opinions. Affections for our friends is usually only a refined form of caring for ourselves.

We say we love our enemy, but deep down in our hearts, we know it isn't true. Our self-love consumes us and we are often unaware.

May the fire of your love enter our hearts and burn up the coil of meanness and hypocrisy so that we may become true disciples.

So, today, we would ask:

- Every mean thought would vanish.
- Every false notion would disappear.
- We turn once again to the truth you have revealed to us through your Son.

Grant mercy upon all of us gathered here; that we might become the quality of mind and heart you so desire. This prayer is offered in the name of pure devotion found in the Lord Jesus Christ.

A Lenten Prayer to Bring Us Closer to the Cross

God of all Seasons – whose story draws near a climax as we approach the cross. In this Season of Lent, O God, we are taught that confession brings us close – and forgiveness sets us free.

We know, O God, that you see each one of us in proximity to the cross. We confess that many of us cannot see the cross from where we live in our lives.

- We have turned our back on your way and are traveling in the wrong direction.
- Our intentions are good, but our habits are bad.
- We are more consumed by maintaining our standard of living than we are of living a righteous and holy life.

Some of us catch a glimpse of the cross every now and then, but we cannot maintain our focus. Our spiritual attention spans are too short and we find ourselves chasing the popular gods of our culture. Some of us have been close to the cross, at times, O God, but the responsibility it demands exceeds our commitment.

Our prayer this day, O God, is for you to show us what it is like for us to live at the foot of the cross.

- Give us a fresh vision that encompasses a life style focused on spiritual values.
- Give us a taste of the joy we share when we choose to live a Christ-like life.
- Give us the courage to stand our ground when temptations challenge our faith.

We come, O God, with so many needs.

- When we are crippled by sickness or disease – be to us the great physician.
- When death robs us of family and friends – be to us the great comforter.
- When we are overcome by life's complexities – be to us our fortress and our strength.

Palm Sunday

Eternal Spirit, our unseen but heart-felt source of peace and power, we gather as your people to offer our praise and thanksgiving.

On this historic day we come with ambivalent feelings. We read of those who lived the streets of Jerusalem, placing pieces of clothing or palm branches in his path—shouting their hosannas! Yet later that week they were singing a different tune.

You know only too well, O God, week after week how we stray from the path you have chosen us to walk.

- Instead of living in harmony with each other, there is often discord and strife.
- We entertain thoughts that are beneath us.
- We say things that we later regret.
- We exhibit actions that betray our life in the Spirit.
- Inspire us with such insight, faith and courage that we will walk the road that makes the difference.
- That we will realize the dangers of being separated from your Spirit.
- That we will realize the hurts we inflict upon others.
- That we will realize that the ways of the world are not your ways.
- Bless us for every example of good will. Bless us for every humane act that offers relief and consolation to our fellow human beings.
- Within our church family, O God, wherever there are hurts, be to us the God who heals.
- Where there is misunderstanding, be to us the God who reconciles.
- Where there is loneliness, be to us the God who comforts and offers meaningful relationship.
- Where there is indecision and apathy, be to us the God who loves and motivates us to right action.

Palm Sunday

Our Father, we gather this day to celebrate the events surrounding Palm Sunday. As we read and hear of Jesus' triumphant entry into Jerusalem, let us feel the excitement of the crowd as they shouted their Hosannas! But also let us feel their shame as they later condemned him.

O God, we are a fickle people. Help us to know in our highest moments we are capable of magnificent worship, but in our lower moments we are a people full of deceit and prone to deny. In our highest moments we embrace the truths of the gospel, but in our lowest moments we confess the cost of discipleship is greater than we are willing to pay.

At the beginning of Holy Week, O God, give us a resolve that will last through Friday, and be born of hope on Easter morning.

Give us the depth of character, a fresh confidence and a bold courage that will keep us faithful to our promise. May the witness of our life not deny our affirmations.

- Enable us to live each day with a gentle and loving spirit.
- Enable us to approach our responsibilities cheerfully and to do our work faithfully.
- Enable us to be kind to friend and foe alike.
- Enable us to be more patient in times of disappointment and less frustration when things do not go well.
- Enable us to accept praise with modesty and criticism without anger.

Give to us the resolution of Jesus when he faced tough decisions; and his singular focus that did not yield to pressure. May the events of the week find us kneeling humbly at the cross on Friday, but anticipating a glorious new beginning on Sunday.

Maunday Thursday Prayer

O God, our journey through Lent has been a journey toward the light of Easter morning; but the journey has also carried us through dark moments and over uncertain paths.

We recall Jesus gathered with his intimate followers to celebrate the Passover, during which He instituted the Sacrament of Holy Communion. Out of the old has come the new.

Help us to realize, O God, the Last Supper was not simply a casual meal, where the mood was jovial, and where normal conversation took place. Rather it was a serious moment in the life of the participants, where each looked the other in the eye and questioned each other's motives.

As we identify with those who were present that evening, so we gather around our own tables, examining our own hearts and minds, knowing we have too often betrayed the cause, deserted a friend, or denied our responsibility.

Help us also to realize, O God, whenever our families gather, large or small, if Christ is present, that meal is indeed holy.

When we dip our bread into the wine, this evening, let it be a solemn occasion when we recommit ourselves to walk from here to the cross as faithful disciples of our Lord.

Good Friday Prayer

Almighty and Everlasting God, whose nature is always to have mercy, you have taught us the greatest love a person can possess is to lay down their life for a friend. But your love is greater still, in that you laid down your life for those who were enemies.

Good Friday stands as a stark reminder of our own waywardness. Good Friday strips us of our pride and deceptive ways. Only when we have forfeited our life will we gain the fruit of your suffering.

O God, enable us to be totally honest. When we consider ourselves to be beyond reproach, confront us with Good Friday.

When we can walk no farther than Gethsemane, remind us of Good Friday.

As we contemplate the last few hours of our Lord's life. Let us experience the kind of death which enables us to be reborn in the likeness of Christ.

In these somber moments, may your sacrificial death turn our nothingness into newness; our darkness into light; our misery into joy; and our death into life.

Let us feel the reality of the crucifixion, so that we will find joy in sacrifice and suffer adversity with patience.

As we experience the crucifixion, let us not blame those who perpetrated this evil deed, but let us look to ourselves as we struggle to understand our own condemnations and rejection. May the shadow of Good Friday cover us until the brightness of Easter Morn.

Easter Sunday

We rejoice, O God, when the women arrived at the tomb early that Sabbath morning, they found they stone had been rolled away. The despair they had felt on Friday suddenly turned to joy.

Help us to realize, O God, we can never be alive to your calling and purpose until the stones in our lives have been rolled away.

There are stones of our own construction which prevent Christ from coming in, as well as stones that impede us from venturing forth to fully embrace the faith.

So, we ask this day, O God, you will roll away the stones which block our spiritual growth; and those which prevent us from actualizing our true human potential.

Roll away the stone of our spiritual arrogance! Let us not think of ourselves more highly than we ought to think. Let us see beyond the boundaries of our own spiritual limitations.

Roll away the stone of our religious indifference! Do not allow any of us to remain apathetic or insensitive. Let the light of the living Christ penetrate the dark and secret places of our dull and listless hearts that we might be cleansed and renewed from within.

Roll away the stone of personal prejudice! Enable us to see all people as your children and heirs of your promise. We confess we do not always call the Jew, Muslim or Buddhist, brother or sister—but you do! Impart to us your heart and mind that we may open wide the doors of understanding and acceptance. Give us loyalty to causes that wrong cannot conquer, and death cannot stop.

The affirmation of Easter is that He Lives! The significance of Easter is we are no longer dead to sin—but alive to Christ!

Thanks be to You, O God, for the note of victory which fills our souls this day.

A Prayer During Eastertide

Eternal God, we give you thanks for the resurrection of our Lord and Savior Jesus Christ. The resurrection is the greatest event in human history.

Take us back in time, O God, to that moment Jest burst forth from the tomb. Nowhere are we told of a single eye witness to this event; yet the stone was rolled away and the tomb was empty.

The proof of the resurrection does not lie in an empty tomb, but in the living presence of a risen Lord.

The season we know as Eastertide is a celebration of the resurrection ongoing within the Christian community. The celebration goes on to-day in the hearts and hopes of the people of the world.

We celebrate this season for a period of fifty days until the Season of Pentecost, which ushers in the Holy Spirit.

Enable us, O God, to celebrate this season with full assurance that eternity follows our earthly existence. The hope of the resurrection is part of the motivation for our living the life of a faithful Christian.

We realize, O God, the resurrection cannot be scientifically proven, but our faith validates the reality of this subjective, heart felt belief.

The study of nature, O God, bears witness that your whole creation is being renewed again and again. The center point of our Christian journey is the assurance that we will live again in the realm of glory.

We are so grateful for this mighty act that enhances our faith to the ultimate. We thank you, O God, for the rewards of a faithful journey.

A Day of Pentecost Prayer

O God, we learn through your sacred scripture that the winds and waves obey your voice. Indeed, all of nature is at your command. We've learned also, O God, that mighty vessels navigate the seas plotting their courses by positions in the stars. May our life's journey find direction by the power above us, around us and in us.

Our greatest temptation is to doubt your love; and one of our greatest stumbling blocks is to believe you are beyond our reach.

We confess, O God, that life in not easy for most of us. The winds and waves of our common problems are much too strong for our fragile vessels. So we ask, O God, be patient in our weaknesses and in our lack of commitment that causes us to drift aimlessly. Steer our ships to quiet harbors where life is safe and peace profound. Set our spiritual compasses to the true and only way. Make us more concerned about the direction we're traveling than our present location.

Give us strength and courage to stay the course. We read that on the day of Pentecost, the Holy Spirit came upon the disciples like the rush of a mighty wind. May that same Spirit come upon us just now bringing a refreshing change to our thinking and behavior. Point us in the heavenly direction and fill our souls with right desires.

As your Spirit blows upon our lives, may it be the influence that speeds our direction to your eternal kingdom. In His name we pray.

(Also available on audio- "Prayers for Daily Living"- Track 3)

Pentecost Sunday

" **G**od of Love and God of Power, grant us in their burning hour grace to ask these gifts of thee, daring hearts and spirits free."

We are grateful, O God, for your word that keeps alive the experience of Pentecost.

We affirm that your energizing Spirit has been in the world since creation – that same Spirit manifesting itself thru the Disciples in a powerful and refreshing way.

May your Power that gave birth to your church be the same power that comes to us today – to renew and re-energize us for ministry.

We pray, O God, that your Presence will shake us out of our complacency. We are a people too often characterized by our luke warmness. We are reminded by your word that we are neither hot nor cold and that you are not pleased with our tepid commitment.

Give us a passion for ministry! On this special anniversary – may we desire above all:

- The power of our convictions of your Gospel truth.
- The power of assurance that claims us as your children and heirs to your promise.
- The power of enablement of the enhancing of our natural gifts and the perfection of our skills needed for effective service.
- Inspire us to sustain what our fore parents began.

Grant us the light to walk by in the dark days.

Grant us the strength to carry the necessary burdens of our human existence.

Grant us the courage to perform Christ-like deeds. Sustain us in our weakest moments. Minister to all of our frailties and enable us to keep true to your purpose for our life and church.

A Prayer During Kingdomtide

God of Peace and Love, we live in a troubled world. Almost every day there is a breaking story of violence on television or in the newspapers.

The church is a broken and shattered institution. We are far from being what you intended us to be, and the sadness of our time is that we don't seem to care.

We are now in the Season of Kingdomtide, a season for us to remember His ministry from birth to death. Easter is behind us, and ahead of us is the challenge of carrying His ministry forward. Each year we should grow stronger and become more enthused about telling His story, and more strengthened to become a more credible witness.

As we look at the early Disciples, we discover that each of them became powerful witnesses of Jesus' death and resurrection. Their compelling witness brought martyrdom to most of them. Enable us to gauge our own faith perspective in the light of their sacrificial witness.

We live in a time that has made us reluctant and ineffective. There is less energy in most congregations to bear witness with a vibrant faith. We are more interested in holding a significant office in the church than we are willing to bear a strong witness of what Christ has done in our life.

Inspire and empower us to carry the faith forward in a bold and fearless way; a way of love, forgiveness and peace, honoring the one who gives us the vision and the power to be the living instrument of God's will in our time.

May we be, for a troubled world, God's faithful presence, so that our prayers may be fulfilled when we pray, "Thy kingdom come, thy will be done on earth as it is in heaven."

Section Two

Prayers for the Church and World

Prayer for the New Year

O God, whose existence stretches to infinity in both directions; who existed before the world began, and who will exist long after everything we know has returned to dust; and who, in your divine plan, has set in motion a process of continual renewal, we worship you who makes all things new.

We confess that eternity is a mystery, for we are so bound to the concept of time. We build our lives around morning and evening, day and night, birthdays and anniversaries, today and yesterday.

As we worship you in this hour, we both celebrate and agonize over the year just passed. We celebrate our victories and agonize over our defeats. A second of our time may be like a thousand years to you, but to us it is a significant part of our life. Let us cherish the memories, and discard the useless.

We are grateful for the time ahead. Prepare us for any disaster, and enable us to make the most of every opportunity.

We affirm, O God, that our spiritual DNA confirms we are your children. Not clones of each other, but your children, unique and special, with the possibility of becoming Christ-like in our thoughts and actions.

Cultivate the spirit within us that responds only to your Spirit.

Put your words in our minds, and your truth in our hearts, so that we may only think and feel that which is true and just.

May our homes become hallowed ground where nothing but love can exist.

May our work places be the dwelling place of the holy where we not only provide for our families, but serve your wider purposes as well.

Let our eyes be focused on the road ahead where no distractions will deter us, and where, at the end of our journey, we will dwell securely in your eternal kingdom.

(Also available on audio- "Prayers for Daily Living"- Track 28)

A New Year's Prayer

"**O** God our help in ages past; our hope for years to come; our shelter from the stormy past and our eternal home."

What a special privilege and joy it is, O God, for all of us as we begin a New Year in your house of worship. We have felt your divine leadership over the past twelve months and our faith makes us confident that you will enable us, not only to survive this new piece of time, but that we will triumph over difficulties yet experienced.

Help us to know, O God, that the greatest enemy we face is our own self-centeredness and our inability to maintain a pure focus on serving your holy will.

- There is so much in our time that distracts us and captures our attention.
- There is so much that offers false hopes only to lead us into disillusionment.
- There is so much that promises us everything, yet the result is disappointment.
- There are powerful gods in our secular culture that seek to claim our ultimate loyalty yet leave us as empty vessels of unfulfilled dreams.

As we begin this New Year, enable us to discern:

- Truth from the falsehoods.
- The real from the artificial.
- Real meaning from shallow, deceiving facades.

Give us a clarity of vision that puts things in proper perspective.

Give us a courageous faith that is willing to dare us to follow our spiritual urgings.

Give us as unblemished loyalty that is not ashamed to bear witness to one Gospel of Love.

For students, O God, give them a positive experience in Education.

For all those who are gainfully employed – give them satisfaction and fulfillment in their work places.

For all of us, O God, give us:

- Good health.
- Pleasing relationships.
- And a pleasant journey in the footprints of our Lord.

A New Year's Prayer

God of all the years that have ever been, we pause in this hour of worship to offer our gratitude for all the good things that you have brought about; and we painfully remember all the things that have been caused by our own neglect and waywordness.

We come with hearts that are heavy for the failures that spoil our recollection of the year past, but we come with hope for the gracious way you will deal with us for this new millennium.

We are grateful for all that crowns life with beauty and blessedness. We offer, thru humble hearts, thanksgiving for family and friends.

We are grateful for all the things that inspire us, and for the many things that sustain us.

Thanks be to thee:

- For the great traditions of our faith that have remained visible and foundational.
- For the faithfulness and wisdom of our fore parents.
- For the visitation of the divine within us where the Christ child dwells.

We pray for our church. Grant us insight and vision as we begin this new and exciting time.

- Show us the possibilities.
- Increase our faith for new commitments.
- Be that constant presence in our lives guiding us to do your will in all things.

Bless those who suffer loss of loved one and bless those who labor under illness or burdens too heavy to bear. Grant us courage for the task before us.

New Promises and Fresh Opportunities

Almighty God, your Psalmist has written before the mountains were brought forth, or ever you had formed the earth and world, from everlasting to everlasting – you are God! We know O God your eternity stretches in every direction. We cannot image a time in which you did not exist and long after this world has returned to dust, you will still be the timeless Creator and Architect of all that remains.

We realize, O God, we are but pilgrims passing through a corridor of time that marks our beginning and end. As earthly creatures our lives are shallow. Our roots lay bare before you. Our lives are fretful and unpredictable. We need your eternal Spirit to infuse our lives with meaning and purpose and give us a perspective of what life would be if we follow the Lord Christ.

We know, O God, each New Year brings new promises and fresh opportunities. Each day can be a new day in your Kingdom that has no end.

For the exciting possibilities of a new future grant us, O God:

- A fresh faith and bold courage with which to face every task.
- Where we have grown discouraged and pessimistic, undergird us with renewed confidence for life's new adventures.
- Teach us that where love is, we find your dwelling place.
- From the ashes of the past year, bring to us the flame of a re-born spirit.
- Send us into your world with restored determinism and a hallowed devotion.

We ask, O God, that you make us adequate, not for tomorrow – but for today. As our fore parents feasted on the manna fresh every morning, may we feed on your Word this day in the spirit of the eternal now.

A Spring Prayer

God of all Seasons, we give thanks for your marvelous creativity and for the many ways you express yourself through nature. Remind us that there is no creation without a creator. We praise your holy name as the one who has brought forth the earth with all its splendor.

As we move from one season to the next, we are grateful for the season past during which growing things have been in wait for the season at hand. For a season, life moved to the roots waiting for the sun and rain to renew the earth. For a season there was something beneath the surface straining to burst forth.

Now, O God, we are experiencing the emergence of new life. We are grateful for the harmony of color with which you clothe the earth. Help us to see the beauty in all living things. The birds sing your song and the plants display your colors.

Let nature speak to us, not of itself, but of the external artist whose brush strokes enable us to view the wonders of your world. We question not the reason for the seasons, but celebrate the one who is the author of it all.

Help us to learn from the lessons of spring!

- Help us to know that renewal is not simply a one-time event –
  · but a process that continues to recycle – ever bringing new/life/ opportunities/ possibilities.
- Renewal of the earth suggests that our life is being renewed again and again – infused with purpose and empowered by your Spirit – to blossom into full maturity in Christ Jesus.

May our life take on a freshness and beauty that reflects our Divine Creator. Whatever our needs, we place them in your hands knowing that one God of Nature is the God who sustains us.

A Mother's Day Prayer

O God, who has created all things and called them good – who ordained marriage as a sacred institution – who invited husband and wife to become co-creators with you – we lift up to you this day the dear and sacred interests of our homes.

Deliver us always, O God, from the secular and spiritual forces that imperil our families:

- Remove from us the ugly moods and foul tempers that endanger our relationships.
- Remove from us any hint of envy, jealousy, or disloyalty.
- Free us up to receive your corrective grace in all of our attitudes.

May every family unit in our church be centers of radiant joy and schools of character. May the love that brought our parents together in their holy covenant be the measure of love that guides our families. May the fruit of our marriage yield up children who are full of grace – who demonstrate godly values – a sense of personal integrity – and examples of holy living.

May this special day in which we honor or remember our mothers. Fill us with inspiration for living the Christ-like life. Give us the spirit of good will and faithfulness.

May all of us be motivated and strengthened to rear our children in the shadow of the Almighty God – knowing that He will provide us with:

- Shade and shelter.
- Care and compassion.
- A right faith.
- A certain hope.
- A Godly patience and a heavenly understanding.

May your love bind us together in a strong fellowship that continues to nourish us in our faith.

A Mother's Day Prayer

Almighty God, who created the world and called it good. We come before your throne of grace this morning affirming your divine assessment of all created things.

- We affirm that life is good and harmonious when we seek to live as you would like us to.
- We affirm that marriage is good when love is the pure essence of our relationships.
- We affirm that children are good because they are a special gift from you.
- We affirm that friendships are good because they are built around a common trust and fidelity.
- We affirm that our vocations and occupations are good because you have given us a way through which our gifts and talents may be expressed.

On this very special day we are grateful for all mothers everywhere.

- We are grateful for their love that has nurtured us in rightful living.
- We are grateful for their patience that is seemingly endless.
- We are grateful for their moral guidance that encourages us to stay on the path of exemplary conduct.
- We are grateful for their loving expectations that keep reminding us of their God-centered hope.

For those mothers who have gone before us, may their remembrance become a hallowed shrine for our thoughts; and for those mothers who are with us now – may their presence be a guiding force in our life. May we never disappoint our mothers!

We pray, O God, for those today who have special requests, whatever the circumstances. Be to all of us that tower of strength, that consoling presence, and the One who can bring to fruition in us the working of your divine plan.

A Prayer for Mother's Day

Almighty God, by whom all the families of earth are named, and who in your wisdom saw fit to bring life into the world and perpetuate it through woman and man. We thank you for the gift of life. Help us always to preserve it, revere it, and respect it at whatever age we find it.

We thank you today for mothers everywhere, from mansion to hut, that they might rear their children under your guidance, and enable them to provide foundation stones of character which will bear much fruit in the days to come.

Bless every home that is represented here this morning. May the parents display a love that comes from a divine relationship. May the children respond to this love in a way the home will become a sacred place for true nurture and development.

Bridge the gulf between the generations, so the adults honor the vigor of the young, and the young revere the wisdom of the old. Help us, through the home, to pass down from generation to generation the spirit of goodness built upon that divine relationship.

Where the home holds an empty chair, let our memories recall joyous and worthy times:

- Where love was fulfilled.
- Where faith became deeper.
- Where hope became dearer.
- And where knowledge we shall meet again and be together becomes clearer.

Bless those who are ill; those who have recently gone through a grief experience; those who are struggling to make a dwelling into a home; and all those who are willing to take on fulfilling relationships.

We put our lives and the lives of our family members in your hands, knowing that you will nurture us to complete fulfillment.

We pray this prayer in the name of one who gave his all; that we might choose to live our life under the umbrella of your divine love and nurture.

A Father's Day Prayer

O God, whose light illumines the universe and whose love satisfies the deep hunger of our heart, we worship you with thanksgiving and joy.

We know, O God, that you require of us a simple faith – like that of little children.

- Enable us to trust as children do.
- Enable us to forgive as easily as children do.
- Instill in us the enthusiasm that so characterizes childhood.

On this special day – we are grateful:

- For all fathers who are earnestly striving to keep the faith.
- For all fathers who are seeking to set a fine example.
- For all fathers who are willing to bear witness to your infinite love.

To all of us, O God:

- Give us a grand vision of what may be, according to your divine expectations.
- Give strength to our hands that we may be able to build, even out of our failures, a fellowship worthy of your Spirit.
- Give us courage in our inward parts that we may keep holy the private places of our own integrity – and to always stand for the dignity of human life.
- Give us a heart of love that crowds out evil thoughts and selfish motives.
- May we hold dear the values of our ancestors that were witnesses for righteous living.

O God, since we last met, some of us have experienced loss, some illness, some loneliness, some failure and disappointment. May your Presence meet us at our point of greatest need.

A Memorial Weekend Prayer

Creator God, once more you have opened the gateway of another morning. Grant us the assurance as surely as the sun rises and sets each day, your love is constant and enduring.

On this special weekend, O God, we give you thanks for a nation that was founded upon the principles of true democracy – where individual freedom and respect for our fellow countrymen are bedrock beliefs. Let us give hearty thanks for all those who have given their lives for those priceless commodities. May this holiday be more than a few days off – but ones filled with admiration for our fallen saints.

We ask, O God, that you deepen our Faith! Where there is doubt – replace it with certainty. Not faith in our own achievements – but in your divine goodness. Enable us, as the church, to preserve the basic tenets of our faith and to keep alive the great traditions of truth and goodness.

We ask, O God, that you quicken our hopes! Save us from the cynicism and skepticism of our present generation. Enable us to see the inherent possibilities of each and every life--to believe that your creation has the possibility of rising above the ordinary to achieve exceptional goals and values.

We ask, O God, that you expand our love!

- Convince us that every life can continue to add new persons to our love list.
- Help us to live above hate, prejudice and vindictiveness.
- Any harsh feeling we may have brought with us – enable us to leave them here and go our way with new respect and a profound love for each other

Make us strong where we are weak. Give us power where we are frail. Where we are timid in our witness, grant to us a fresh boldness and undying love and sympathy for each other.

God and Country

Eternal God, our Father, who has created us with minds capable of discerning truth, with hearts capable of loving not only ourselves, but others, and with wills capable of choosing righteousness.

We bring before your throne of grace our anxieties, our doubts, our fears, and our tendency of wanting to place our will above your will. We echo the words of the Apostle Paul, "things we should do, somehow we cannot, and things that we should not do, we find ourselves doing."

Grant us, O God, the insight to see the harm done through our own neglect and carelessness. May we learn that no matter how private our sin, or how small it seems in consequences, we hold back the advancement of your kingdom.

O God, we ask that you would throw your arms around our country and its leaders.

Enable them to lead with wisdom and compassion. Bring us together in perfect harmony. Give to all of us a clear vision, a clarity of how a nation responds to being "under God." Bring us swift answers to complex problems. We pray that our democratic process will be faithful to our Constitution, and loyal in our servanthood.

O God, you have blessed us with great resources. May all of us accept our stewardship responsibilities. May we give generously, not grudgingly. May we experience the joy that comes from being unselfish, and may our commitment be equal to the cause of Christ.

Bless all of us who have special requests. May our church bear constant witness to the power and goodness of our Lord and Savior, Jesus Christ.

A Fall Prayer

O God, creator of the universe and of everything good and beautiful, we pause in gratitude this day for your mercy that redeems, and for your loving nature that satisfies our deepest need.

- We are grateful for the rain that replenishes our reservoirs and gives new life to living things.
- We are grateful for fall weather that brings a refreshing coolness to our land that signals the changing of the season.
- We are grateful for the diversity of the seasons, all the while bearing witness to the continuity of your ever changing forms.

We offer our petitions that mirrors our needs.

- We bring before you our personal needs.
- Our physical needs for shelter, food and recreation.
- Our spiritual needs to be filled with your Spirit that offers peace within, and gives us confidence without.
- For family values that are primary.

We bring to you the needs of our neighbor. We pray for secure relationships, for meaningful work and refreshing leisure time, and for all of us to share in significant worship. May our needs be met with an outpouring of your grace.

We bring to you the needs of our church.

- We pray for loyal worshippers, for the development of the holy habits of study, prayer, fasting and stewardship.
- We pray for your church here that welcomes the stranger and serves the needs.

We pray for the needs of our country.

- We pray that our leaders would possess a great vision.
- We pray that our leaders would strive to become morally righteous, and set an exemplary standard.
- We pray that our leaders will be compassionate, and seek to serve the public good.

May our worship this day pay homage to your divine guidance, and may our hopes for the world be affirmed by diligent and loving service.

A Prayer of Thanksgiving

Eternal God, whose love knows no limit and whose goodness the underserving as well as the deserving experience in equal measure – we pause before your throne of grace this morning with praise and thanksgiving on our lips.

We are grateful for the good earth out of which our sustenance comes. For seedtime and harvest that keeps your beauty before us – we remember this season especially.

We remember with grateful hearts

- The homes that provided shelter, warmth, and love
- We remember the hours of parental investment in us
- And how, at times, we ignored it and seemed so ungrateful.

We give you thanks for a nation that has been blessed beyond measure. One that has labored long to become the model for democracy for the world.

- We pray for the leaders of our land
- May their honesty match their responsibility
- Grant them wisdom and the time to be able to make the right · decision in a time of uncertainty.

We are exceedingly grateful for the church.

- For the revelation of your love expressed through our lord and savior, Jesus Christ
- For the truth of his life and his own sacrificial spirit.

We are grateful for the saints of our day.

- Who have planted the seeds of truth in our own hearts
- Who have demonstrated love
- Who model the hope of your future kingdom.

Help us to realize as we gather together this day that thanksgiving must be expressed in thanks living. May we learn to express our faith through kind and benevolent acts of love.

In Remembrance of 9/11

Creator God, you have given us the capacity to remember the past, but without the ability to see into the future. You have shaped our lives, both by the past and the future. We are driven by past events, and we are pulled into the future as we link ourselves to your purpose and plan.

Our lives are shaped by the journeys we take, by which road we follow. Our detours remind us of our weaknesses and lack of commitment.

This week, O God, we have been painfully reminded of the events of 9/11. To view the film clips and to recall the tragic events of years past, we are reminded of the fragility of the human mind, and the corruptness of the human heart, when it is controlled by selfish and evil forces.

We solemnly remember those who lost their lives:

- Some in heroic situations.
- Some who simply happened to be in the wrong place at the wrong time.
- Some because of false teachings that corrupted their hearts.
- But none gave their life because God willed it to happen.

So we come today, O God, bruised and broken by the calamities of the past. Seeking forgiveness for acts small and large, where we have infringed upon another's liberty.

- Save us from evil desires.
- Save us from wrong choices.
- Save us from ever coveting anything that is our neighbors.

Set our feet on Ministry Road. Put your Word in our minds and your Truth in our hearts.

We know that our journey will not always be smooth or inviting. There will always be rough waters, rocky roads, and turbulent skies. But as we walk Ministry Road, let it be for us an Emmaus experience.

A Post-9/11 Prayer

Almighty God, whose love encompasses all humankind, whose compassion is without question, yet One who hold us responsible for our actions. We turn to you now as a part of your fractured world realizing that relationships, at all levels, are in need of healing and restoration.

We realize, O God, that our Constitution reflects your divine wisdom – that our population is diverse in race, religion and culture – that respect for human life is our sacred responsibility because every human being is an expression of your divine creation.

We realize, O God, that grace does not come cheaply, neither does our freedom. The receiving of your gracious acts requires us to respond in perfect obedience. To live in freedom is to desire that all persons become free – politically, socially, and spiritually.

Search out the hidden motives of our hearts and remold us in your image.

- Teach us what it means to be faithful! Enable us to submit ourselves as holy and living sacrifices to your will.
- Teach us what it means to be courageous! To stand for what is right, true and holy and never flinch in our duty.
- Teach us what it means to be united! May all of your children come to know that there is but one way to live; that our actions are expressions of one heart and will.
- Teach us what it means to live in Peace! May our conflicts cease. May we learn to live as brothers and sisters under One God – Father of us all.

We ask, O God, that you bring us to ground zero spiritually. Enable us to build and maintain a foundation around that which is genuine, permanent and godly. May love be the force that rules all humankind! In the name of one who was love incarnate.

(Also available on audio- "Prayers for Daily Living"- Track 6)

In the Face of War and Terrorism

God of infinite knowledge, who seeks to impart your truth to our finite minds; God, of perfect love, who seeks to express yourself to an imperfect people; God, who makes available your power to a humanity who craves power, but lacks the wisdom and integrity to use it correctly, we pause in these sacred moments, to reflect upon your gracious acts and your loving ways.

Our hearts are heavy, O God, with the talk of war. We realize that, at times, war is inevitable. But is it so now? Speak clearly and forcefully to the leaders of world governments about the necessity of military engagement. Be especially with our own President as he seeks peaceful solutions. Help all of us to know, beyond any doubt, when the time comes to stop talking and start shooting. We pray that there will be no innocent blood on our hands.

We confess, O God, many of us are running scared because of terroristic threats. We are overwhelmed with the uncertainty of where and when the enemy will strike next. We realize there is some cause for alarm, but is it possible for us to find true security in duct tape or a gas mask? Grant us a spiritual calmness that enables us to function effectively even amid the turmoil and uncertainty of perilous times.

We are grateful for the good news of Scripture which affirms that God is on our side. But the great question of our humanity is, whose side are we on? We struggle for answers to complex questions. We are over our head and we know it. We need your divine guidance and assistance.

The Scripture teaches us that Salvation comes when, in faith, we respond to your grace. Help us to realize that Christianity is a two-way street. Your call is clear, our response is in question. Your purpose is our guiding light, but we too often choose to live in darkness.

Our world is in critical condition. We need your loving and stabilizing grace to encircle the hearts of the world's people that we may live in perfect peace.

We pray for all sorts and conditions of people. Be with the sick, the bereaved, the lonely, the disappointed, the misguided and those of a fragile faith. May your love and power transform all of us into faithful effective disciples.

A Prayer Concerning Possible War

O God, who dwells in high places, yet one who visits those of low estate. We come with praise on our lips, but with lives needing you cleansing and renewing presence.

Lift our visions beyond our own personal horizons, and enable us to catch a glimpse of your creation from your perspective.

- Our accepted world is too small.
- Our interests are focused inward.
- And our commitments lack the intensity to serve your larger challenges.

Elevate our thinking, O God, that we may entertain only pure thoughts and highest ideals. Purify our minds and sharpen our focus. Help us to build our lives on the Rock of our Salvation – none other than the One who ascended to your heavenly throne.

Elevate our level of commitment. Motivate us by spiritual longings rather than by earthly attractions.

O God, we bring so many concerns:

- Soften the heart of ruthless dictators – so that war would be unnecessary.
- Let us resort to war only after all diplomacy fails.
- If war is our best option, protect our military from deadly chemicals or conventional engagements.
- Give all world governments a passion for peace, and may they speak with a single voice.

In our homes and communities – there are local needs and private concerns:

- Comfort all who are greatly affected.
- Heal all who suffer from physical malady, emotional stress or spiritual brokenness.
- Befriend all who are lonely.
- Lessen the anxieties that render us incapable.

By the power of your love, remold us in the image of Christ and redirect our steps that we may follow the way of the cross.

A Time of War

God of Peace, who desires that all your children dwell in perfect harmony, we turn to you in the crisis of the world's condition. We are burdened with the tragic consequences of a failed diplomacy, and our hearts are heavy with the decision to send our troops into battle.

We realize, O God, that the wages of war are never good. Let us mourn over the lives that will be lost, many of them innocent, soldier and civilian alike. Let us mourn the money spent for bullets instead of bread. Let us mourn the hardships that will be endured by all affected.

Be with our President as he walks the lonely road of leadership. May your wisdom guide him in his thinking, and your strength empower him in his actions. Let us not be divided as a people who share a common heritage. Let us model a democracy that will show the world's people how to live and govern.

Be with the leaders of other governments, that they would be guided by higher principles than their own national interest. May the nations of the world work together for the common good. Soften the hearts of despotic leaders everywhere. May their motivation be for the welfare of their people and nation, rather than serving their own selfish desires.

We pray for a swift victory and for an orderly withdrawal of our troops, when the time is right to do so. May the civilian population receive humane treatment, and be allowed to establish a government that serves its own people well, and its neighbors with dignity.

Protect our service men and women from the unknown dangers they will be facing. May the loss of life be minimal, and the fruit of their involvement be a peace that brings stability to the Middle East, and around the world. May no life be lost in vain.

Convince us, O God, that the seeds of war are sown in personal disputes. Turn us from the grudges we have borne; from the unbrotherliness we have practiced; and from the selfishness we have clung to.

May the hearts of the world's people be bound up in prayer until a peaceful and lasting solution comes in our time and in every spot on the face of the earth.

A Post-9/11 Prayer

Almighty God, who has created this vast universe, and who has set the planets in their orbit – yet one who graciously allowed our fore parents to establish this great country founded on the principles of democracy, with freedom being the chief cornerstone.

We turn to you now imploring you to undergird us with divine wisdom and power.

- Our minds are clouded with an overload of information, with too little true knowledge.
- Our hearts are heavy with grief and torn with conflicts that threaten to undermine our faith.
- Left to our own resources, our opinions are too biased and our judgments too harsh.

We realize, O God, regardless of religion, race, or culture, all of us are guaranteed the right to worship as we choose. Keep us from mass condemnation and from panic in the street that tend to give birth to a vigilante justice. Keep us from any expression of freedom that is short sighted and inappropriate.

We trust you, O God, and we pray that you will guide our thoughts and direct our actions. We pray for those who have lost their lives and their families who mourn. We pray for our President and for leaders of governments around the world. May all of them gain the vision of what needs to be done. May their choices be clear and their resolve strengthened. Once they know the right thing to do, may they do it in faith that it is your will.

May the banner of freedom be lifted up in such a way that it would give light to other nations and peoples in their struggle for justice and peace. Confirm our solidarity. Quicken our resolve. Let us be slow to anger but abounding in steadfast love. May our actions be in keeping with your holy will.

Prayer for Armed Forces Day

Eternal God, Father of those who wish for freedom; but especially those who are willing to lay down their life in order to keep our country safe. In today's world it is very difficult to know our friends from our enemies.

Regardless of the ambiguity, keep our men and women safe wherever they serve, whether on land, sea or air. We are grateful for their courage and willingness to serve in a time so unpredictable.

On the occasion of this day, make those of us who serve in the defense of our county more aware of the sacred trust and privilege that is ours. Instill into the hearts of all who serve a sense of righteousness in their duty, and a resolve not to comprise with those whose values clash with ours.

We are aware, O God, of the horrors of the battlefield, but we are rewarded by the safety of those who are not engaged in actual conflict. You have made of one blood all the nations and peoples of the earth. We pray for the day when all wars will cease, peace will settle over us like a comforting breeze.

Let each one of us rededicate ourselves to the ideal of a peaceful co-existence, while at the same time maintaining a vigilance against all forms of aggression, knowing we have the right, and perhaps the duty, to maintain our country amid all kinds of hate and threatening engagement.

Let there be peace on earth, O God, and let it begin with each one of us.

War and Natural Disasters

O God, whose heart must surely be broken, because of the unfortunate tragedies that have plagued your world. Some of the tragedies have been fueled by human anger and greed, while others are at the mercy of nature out of control.

The wars of this world seem to be hopeless situations. How many lives must be lost before peace can be found? There are people who share the same heritage, who speak the same language, who supposedly worship the same God, yet they wreak havoc on each other's lives. It seems to us that life is cheap in that part of the world, and honor has no place. We believe, O God, that people can be changed; that we can be neighborly regardless of ethnic origin or clan identification. May their swords be turned into plowshares, and their spears into pruning hooks.

O God, we also witness the mighty force of nature when it is out of control-leaving death and destruction in its wake. Bless especially the poor and homeless. Your children have suffered grievous losses, many without means to rebuild.

We are often without explanation when bad things happen to the undeserved, except to affirm that natural disasters are not heaven sent as a punishment upon those who did not live by the dictates of Your Book. The laws of disaster have plausible reasons, but your wrath is not one of them. We worship one whose motive is never retaliation or revenge, but one whose passion is fueled by love.

Grant to all of us a spirit of compassion and generosity, and a willingness to do whatever we can until life returns to normal for the displaced.

Prayers for Politics/Elections

O God, whose divine character is shrouded in mystery, yet whose love is clearly expressed in Jesus the Christ.

We realize, O God, to be human is to experience the problems and joys of our finite existence. Life is often fragile. For some of us questions of health robs us of a full and joyful life. Members of our church family, even now, are undergoing tests to better define their medical condition. We pray always, for an accurate diagnosis, and effective treatment. May our health professionals draw from your divine wisdom, as they seek to provide holistic answers to our medical questions.

Some of us, O God, live under the cloud of economic uncertainty. Some of us lack job security. Many of us carry heavy debt loads. Grant us insight into our economic condition, and the ability to gain control of our situation.

Some of us, O God, need domestic tranquility and family solidarity. Enable us to strengthen the bonds of our marriage covenant, and may we train our children in the way they should go, knowing that seeds planted today will bring forth good fruit in the years to come.

We have grown tired, O God, of political campaigning. We are called upon to exercise our right to vote. May we do so responsibly. Give us greater clarity on the issues that drive our candidates. May those who can lead our country the best, be clear winners.

May each of us now express our needs for today and our hopes for tomorrow.

Prayers for Scouting or Secular Organizations

Eternal God, who is high above us, yet somehow within us, we gather in your presence to offer our gratitude for our many blessings.

We experience your grace in so many ways and in so many places that it becomes difficult for us to express how we feel. We are grateful for life itself, for the many relationships we hold dear, for the love we experience in our home, for sacrifices made and love demonstrated so clearly and generously.

We are grateful for the church that continues to be the meat and bread to our spiritual bodies. We are grateful for the gospel being presented with courage and conviction, for music that stirs our soul and inspires us with its sound and sense, and for those who give of themselves so unselfishly, with their possessions as well as their personalities.

We are grateful for all of the programs and organizations that supplement and compliment the Gospel of Christ. We are grateful for the Scouting Program that challenges young minds and motivates our youth to higher ideals. We are grateful for the character building this organization promotes and demonstrates.

Come close to us in our personal trouble. Relieve those hearts that are heavy. Remove the anxieties from those who face difficult times. Strengthen those who face overwhelming temptation. According to our needs, may the riches of your grace empower all of us who seek to serve your Holy will.

A Prayer for Marriage and Family

O God, who created us male and female, and who created us for each other; may the personal uniqueness of each, find completeness in the other.

We affirm, O God, that the marriage covenant was established by You, giving us the most intimate of all relationships, where our differences are celebrated in the two becoming one.

Within our holy covenant, may there always be:

- Equality in our marriages.
- A dual devotion to common objectives.
- Relationships free from any kind of abuse.
- And a proper balance between freedom and responsibility.

We are grateful, O God, for the gift of parenthood. For the ability and opportunity to bear children, and to rear them in the atmosphere of Your divine community.

- Enable us to give shape to their faith and character.
- May we receive the gift of parenthood as a joy rather than a burden.
- Let us affirm that, within the family, no member is less important than the other.

As we worship this day, and prepare to live in your world as faithful followers, may there always be:

- The highest integrity for the individual.
- Fidelity in our marriages.
- A productive and rewarding relationship with our children.
- And may we discover the joy in all circumstances.

A Funeral Prayer for a Mother

Almighty God, Father and Creator of us all, we acknowledge that you have created us. You have sustained us through times of toil and trouble. And when we breathe our last, you claim us for eternity. We are grateful for the memories we hold dear:

- For all the relationships through which we have matured.
- For the love of parents who nurtured us and instilled in us the values of life that are essential as we live in community.
- For the affections of friends who have stood by us and shouldered our burdens.
- For the church which has been the meat and bread of our spiritual bodies.

Our life may be taken but memories remain.
We are grateful for the Promises of Scripture.

- Grateful for the truth and power of the gospel as it assures us of life eternal.
- Grateful for your Spirit who witnesses to our spirit that we are children of the Most High God.
- And that this dear mother and friend who rests even today in the arms of God.

Give us the strength of character and the boldness of spirit that we can testify as our Lord overcame the grave he has made it possible for all of us to share this eternal bliss.

A Funeral Prayer for a Woman

Eternal God, from whom we come, to whom we belong, and in whose service is our peace, even in the presence of death, our first word is to give you thanks for your unnumbered mercies.

- For the memory of loved ones now departed, in whom we have seen the light of your presence – we offer our thanks.
- For victories of character over trial, of courage over difficulty, of faith over sorrow – we offer our thanks.

We affirm, O God, that you are the God of the living as you did not lose (name) in giving her to us. Make us aware that we do not lose her in giving her back to you. Deepen our faith, O God, in life eternal.

We are grateful for the legacy that (name) leaves with us, both physical and spiritual.

- For the gifts and talents that were hers, that she so generously shared.
- For the sweetness of spirit.
- For the genuineness of character.
- For her unquestionable devotion to You and to her church.

Enable all of us who mourn her departure to have:

- An abiding memory that will inspire and comfort us.
- A faith that conquers all.
- A peace that calms our fears and offers us a quiet assurance, even though our hearts are heavy, we know that all is right within our world – and that (name) rests in the arms of God.

This prayer we offer in the name of Him who have fulfilled his promise "that where I am, you will be also".

A Prayer for Older Adults

O God, our Heavenly Father, whose gift is our length of days, help us to make the noblest use of body and mind in our advancing years. According to our strength, apportion our work, that we shall continue to be effective.

As you have pardoned our transgressions, may the memory of time wasted grow dim and may the good we have accomplished shine forth clearly.

We are grateful for the gifts you have given us, although we have failed to put them to full use in every endeavor. Our stamina and vision have grown weaker and dimmer, yet our gratitude has not wavered.

You have given us many good friends who live on both sides of the great divide. We cherish the ones left standing, and we miss terribly the ones who have gone on before us. Life has been rich and full, and the friendships we have shared have added a tremendous dimension to our work and leisure moments.

Even at our age, keep us employed at the work you have so graciously provided. Give us visions of what lies ahead, to keep us busy with tasks undone, and keep us healthy that we may yet fulfill an even greater role in this awesome thing we call our given responsibility.

Enable us to bear our infirmities with optimism and a cheerful patience. Keep us from narrow pride in outgrown ways, and a vision that still motivates us in service.

Let thy peace rule our spirits through all the trials of waning powers. Take from us the fear of death, that with glad hearts, we my serve your holy name with love and thanksgiving until we breathe our last breath. Receive us into your arms of mercy echoing the words: "Well done, good and faithful servant."

A Prayer for Those Going to the Holy Land

O God, we affirm the words of your Psalmist: "Your Word is a lamp to our feet and a light to our path." Your light, O God, has overcome the darkness of our own sin and ignorance, and your lamp has illumined the way we should walk.

Your Word, O God, has become our teacher and example.

- It is in your Word that we discover your loving and gracious nature.
- It is in your Word that the message of the prophets become relevant in our time.
- It is in your Word that we can assess our natural worth.
- It is your Word that governs our relationship to each other.

May your Word be clear to us this day as we seek to understand and do your will.

Our prayer this day, O God, is a special petition for those in our congregation who will make their pilgrimage this week to your Holy City and Land. May this be for them an experience unexcelled in their faith journey. May their travel be safe, their encounters inspiring, and as they walk the Via Dolorosa may it remind them of the walk to Emmaus, where they sense the presence of the living Lord.

We pray this day for every sort and condition of persons.

- May those who suffer illness see the reality of a healthier condition.
- May those who are bereaved sense the presence of a blessed companionship.
- May those who are struggling with difficult situations experience a smoother path and a more peaceful journey.

Communion

Almighty God, ever present and ever loving, we confess there are time in our life when you seem so far away that you are beyond our reach. We say our prayers that mirror our needs, but they often seem not to go beyond where we are.

We know in our minds that you are constantly with us, seeking to draw us into the most intimate of all relationships. Yet in our heart we know we are the ones who have retreated into our own private corners.

Help us to realize, O God, that the meeting place where our spirits come together, most completely, is at your holy altar, our holy of holies. Help us to remember:

- It was at your holy altar we exchanged our marriage vows— pledging to live out our lives in conformity with your holy discipline.
- It was at your holy altar we celebrated the baptism of our off-springs, seeking to rear our children in this divine community.
- It has been at your holy altar we have paid last respects to our loved ones, committing them into your sacred care.
- It has been at your sacred altar we have participated again and again in the Sacrament of Holy Communion.
- It is at your sacred altar that our lives have been renewed again and again.

So, we come again this day to participate in this holy drama, remembering the life, death and resurrection of our Lord.

Let us feel the magnet of your holy love as it pulls us toward that sacred relationship, where life is renewed and sustained.

Your presence in our lives can heal our every wound, and lift our sagging spirits.

(Also available on audio- "Prayers for Daily Living"- Track 9)

Communion Day Prayer

O God, whose light illumines the universe and where truth enlightens our minds, we confess to be children of the light, but we find ourselves walking in darkness and while we confess to be followers of the truth, our lives deny our affirmation.

May the light of your countenance so penetrate our inner being that all of our secret shadows will disappear, and may the reality of your truth purge away every temptation to follow the false gods of our culture.

O God, once our life has been changed by the miracle of your grace, may we discover the truth and goodness of your diving character. May we find that purpose for which we were created. Enable us to worship you without ceasing, and to serve you with an unflinching loyalty.

Give us the strength of body and health of mind to worship you graciously and generously.

- May we be deeply moved by another's pain.
- May we be genuinely affected by another's sorrow.
- May we be touched by another's loneliness.
- May we be motivated by the poverty of another's social conditions.
- May we be so conditioned through worship and prayer that we will be move from a pious solitude to a Christian attitude of benevolent response.

Enable us to realize that the harvest will never be reaped until we become reapers. Condition us, O God, for action.

May our time at the table this day be a time of true repentance and deep commitment.

Communion- Imperfection Swallowed Up by Forgiving Love

Almighty God, by your wisdom you brought order out of chaos; by your power you raised our Lord Jesus from the dead; and by your grace you are willing to forgive us of our sin.

There are so many things for which we should confess:

- For careless words spoken that have defamed the character of another person.
- For random acts of selfishness that have offended our neighbors.
- For opportunities we have wasted and for many whom we have neglected.
- We have a way of giving first class loyalties to second class causes – and we have suffered the consequences of our choices.

By your grace, O God, meet us in the secret placed of our hearts and remove all those things that drag us down and prevent us from being our best.

We long for the assurance experienced by the Psalmist when he wrote: "That as far as the East is from the West – so far does he remove our transgressions from us."

As we meet at the table this morning, let our imperfections be swallowed up by your forgiving love and may we be empowered to live victoriously in His resurrection faith.

We pray, O God, for all sorts of conditions of persons:

- For those who find healing difficult – lay your hand of comfort upon them.
- For those who find separation painful – may your presence offer reconciliation and peace.
- For those who struggle with unseen enemies – may your presence be a heartfelt experience that witnesses to a divine friendship.

A Confession on Communion Sunday

O Lord, our God, whose glory is written across the heavens, yet whose greater glory is to dwell within the human heart. We pause in this sacred hour to offer our praise and thanksgiving.

When we consider your majesty and your infinite goodness, O God, our hearts are hushed. Our souls bow in silence realizing that we have fallen short of your divine expectations.

We confess that we experience different levels of alienation – from you and from each other. We experience so many emotions that threaten our spiritual stability.

- Where there is guilt over acts committed, may they be confessed.
- Where there is anguish over personal problems, may we, with assurance, find adequate solutions.
- Where there is conflict, in all of our relationships, may the path of peace be discovered.
- Where there is sorrow over the loss of a family member or a friendship, may our loneliness be met with genuine companionship.

As we gather for the Holy Meal this morning may we experience the joy of being found, forgiven and restored.

Give us as a reward for our worship – an hour of spiritual communion – so rich and rewarding – that our lives will be changed, our intentions grounded in a genuine faith that can lead us to live victoriously in the life and ministry of Jesus Christ.

Renewal of Baptism

Eternal God, in whom there is no beginning or end, no daylight or darkness, who is the same yesterday, today and forever, we stand in need of your renewing presence and forgiving love.

Grant that, in this hour of worship, we may rediscover the kind of faith that overcomes the world. We realize that we do not live by bread alone, but by every word proceeding from your mouth. Make us quick to remember the homes that have nourished us, friends who have sustained us, and experiences that have inspired and motivated us.

Beneath the daily stress of ordinary living, grant us a full measure of serenity and steadfastness; that we will be like the man who built his house upon the rock.

- Give us courage, in your Spirit, to be generous, unafraid, and truthful.
- Enable us to face life's situations with confidence and strength.
- Lay before us a vision worthy of your calling.
- Let us see clearly the path you have chosen for us to follow.
- May the renewal of our baptism enable us to be exemplary witnesses of the risen Christ.

We pray for all sorts and conditions of persons.

- Bless those who suffer any form of illness or disease.
- Bless those who suffer any kind of loss, family, friend or property.
- Bless those who have difficult decisions to make.

Before we leave this place of worship, may we faithfully resolve to walk your way, with the assurance that you will walk with us in our daily journey.

Stewardship or Capital Campaign Prayer

O, God, our cups overflow with the blessings you have so freely given us; and your grace is a constant reminder of your matchless love and forgiving nature.

We realize, O God, we are on the receiving end of so many of your blessings, that it seems our heart would surely burst if we did nothing to pass them on.

When we take an inventory of our earthly possessions, we discover how few of them exist that are gained through our own ingenuity. Now is the time to declare our dependence upon the One who is wholly accessible and overwhelmingly generous.

Grant to us, O God, a genuine enthusiasm for the sharing of our gifts. Let our practice of sharing earthly treasures, truly reflect a new level of faith and commitment. Let us never fool ourselves by saying that we are giving from our abundance, when we are really giving a portion of what is left after we have paid our earthly dues.

Your desire for us, O God, is that we enjoy the abundant life. You have taught us, that the abundant life is not one saturated with material possessions, but a spiritual fullness that overflows with joy.

We pray for those in our church family who suffer from any kind of illness; or who may be living in a state of high anxiety over private and personal matters; or who may be struggling over how they will respond to the challenge of our campaign. May your spirit guide us in all matters, and may our commitment be pleasing in your sight.

Ground Breaking Prayer

On this day, O God, we declare that we are one family, under one roof – led by one Spirit, serving one purpose. Bless the contributions that have been made that make this day possible.

May those unable to be here, be one in the Spirit with us.

O God, you have entrusted to us your church and your ministry.

- May our minds be enlightened.
- May our hearts inspired.
- May our hands made able and our spirits willing to carry out your work.

We affirm that the ground on which our building is to be built is indeed Holy Ground. On this sacred soil we pledge ourselves to praise your Holy Name and to spread your eternal word. May the turning of the soil symbolize the turning of our lives over to you.

Help us to build your church upon the cornerstone of our faith – Jesus Christ our Lord. May the plumb line of His nature and character be the model for our ministry.

May every brick or stone that is laid represent every member family of our congregation. May every particle of construction represent the totality of your congregation here committed to do your Holy will.

May the mortar that holds these stones together be none other than:

- The truth of your Holy Scriptures.
- The power of your Holy Spirit binding us together – giving us one witness genuine and powerful – that all who drive by this place will know that we are Christians by our love.

May the quality of our ministry reflect the one who was the incarnation of grace, love, and truth.

Ground Breaking Prayer

On this day, O God, we declare that we are indeed one family, under one roof, led by one Spirit, and serving one purpose. Bless the contributions that have been made that makes this day possible. May all those who are unable to be here this day, be one in the Spirit with us.

O God, you have entrusted to us your church and your ministry. May our minds be enlightened, our hearts inspired, our hands made able, and our spirits willing to carry out your work.

We affirm that the ground on which we build is indeed holy ground. On this sacred soil we pledge ourselves to praise your Holy Name and to spread your eternal word. May the turning of the soil symbolize the turning of our lives over to you.

Help us to build your church upon the cornerstone of our faith, Jesus Christ our Lord. May the plumb line of his nature and character be the model for our ministry. May every brick or stone that is laid represent every member and family of our congregation. May every particle of construction represent the gifts and talents of our members committed to do your holy will.

May the mortar that holds these stones together be none other than:

- The truth of your Holy Scriptures
- The power of your Holy Spirit, binding us together, giving us one witness, genuine and powerful, that all who drive by this place will know that we are Christians by our love.

May the quality of our ministry reflect the one who was the incarnation of grace, love and truth.

Consecration of Building

"**O** God our help in ages past, our hope for years to come; our shelter from the stormy past and our eternal home!"
We have so much, O God, for which to be grateful:

- For this piece of earth that has become sacred soil to us.
- For a beautiful and functional facility where the saints can be equipped and enabled to carry out our mission.
- For the sacrificial gifts and efforts of all those who have made contributions, in whatever form, to realize this phase of our dream.

We add, O God, you enable us to be true to the purpose for which this building was constructed:

- For the reading and preaching of Your Holy Word
- For Christian teaching and nurturing of all those who pass through those doors
- For praising you through music
- For the fellowship that binds us together as brothers and sisters in Christ, and for the support and encouragement we receive from each other.

Empower us, O God, to measure up to the challenges of the future.

- May every service conducted, every act performed be the one that offers your praise and thanksgiving.
- Through every person baptized, may we realize the call and affirmation of Almighty God.
- May all who repeat their sacred vows realize that their marriage is to act out the mandate of love.

- When we gather in memory of one of our devoted family members, may we realize the influence of our witness, and be strengthened to proclaim the Gospel of Christ to those in our community.
- May the power and the memory of the day inspire and challenge us as we seek to serve our Holy will.

Prayer for the Consecration of a Worship Space

Almighty God, our hearts are overflowing with gratitude as we gather for the opening of this new facility. It is fitting that the initial service should be one of worship, where your name is exalted above every name. Our hearts echo the refrain: "Surely the presence of the Lord is in this place."

We are grateful for all those who have labored long and hard to bring this project to fruition. But let us, in humility, confess that it was not our labors alone that made all of this possible, rather we celebrate the guiding and sustaining presence of your Spirit which enabled us to achieve this marvelous work.

We are exceedingly thankful to have a facility that can accommodate many activities, yet with only one purpose in mind, to bring individuals into an active relationship with our Lord and Savior, Jesus Christ.

Make us aware that with new facilities, comes new responsibilities. Empower us to meet the challenges of the future with grace and a humble dedication. May every activity held in this building bring honor and glory to your most holy name.

Grant to this congregation always, a clarity of vision; a certainty of mind and heart; a devotion to duty; and the will to bring our life into harmony with your will, that we may live out our days with confidence, boldness and with a divine perseverance.

May the excitement of this day never fade, and may our labors never fail, as we seek to serve your high and holy purposes.

Worship in New Facility

"This is the day that the Lord has made, let us rejoice and be glad in it."

Almighty and Eternal God, our hearts are overflowing with gratitude as we gather for worship in this beautiful new facility. Our hearts echo the refrain "Surely the presence of the Lord is in this place."

We are grateful for all those who have labored long and hard to bring this project to fruition. Let us, in humility, confess that it was not our labors alone that made all this possible. Rather we celebrate the guiding and sustaining presence of your Spirit that enabled us to achieve this marvelous work.

Make us aware, O God, that with new facilities comes new responsibilities. Convince us that we will be able to do great things, if we will submit ourselves to your leadership. Grant us such clarity of vision, independence of mind, and courage of will that we may live our lives with confidence, boldness and perseverance.

Bless those in our church family who could not be here this morning. We pray for every sort and condition of persons:

- Bless those who labor under illness, disease or misfortune.
- Bless those who are bereaved because of loss.

Grant us the inspiration of the Holy Spirit that we may become that city set in a hill, where others may see our faithful works and where we may be found, at all times, glorifying your Holy Name.

Church Anniversary Prayer

Almighty and everlasting God, Creator of all worlds, yet the giver of each individual gift – we pause before your throne of grace this morning realizing that we, too often, call upon you with words neatly chosen, but with hearts greatly removed.

In days of old, O God, whenever your people desired to be in your presence, they would come to the Tent of Meeting. We have been to the tomb this morning and we have felt your mighty presence through the fellowship of each other.

Now we come to your sacred altar to worship you in spirit and in truth.

- To worship a powerful God is to reap a powerful fellowship.
- To worship a loving God is to reap a community of people who share their love with those in the church as well as those in the community.
- To worship a generous God, who has no boundaries in the sharing of your goodness, we reap a community of people who have developed generous hearts as they respond to your need.

Remind us, O God, you called together a group of faithful, devoted followers. You planted a seed of what was possible. And today you are reaping a harvest from the first fruits of those who chose to be faithful.

You have been so good to us, O God.

- You have blessed our labors with greater numbers.
- You have blessed our labors with remarkable achievements.
- You have blessed our labors with a powerful vision and a dedication to see your dreams become a reality.

We pray, O God, you will continue to underwrite our vision with your presence that will move us to that day when all of our lives will be holy and blameless, and that the church on earth will be your divine instrument in the salvation of humankind.

Church Anniversary Celebration Prayer

O God, who surely delights in the assembly of your people; we gather, this day, to offer our praise and thanksgiving, to One who is altogether Holy.

Today is a special day of reunion and celebration, one filled with rich and meaningful memories, as well as, one filled with challenging opportunities.

We are grateful for those persons, 10 years ago, who were willing to take on a task much larger than their limited vision ever imagined. We acknowledge:

- Their commitments were sincere.
- Their labors diligent.
- Their hopes built around the dream God had planted in their hearts.

And now we reap the harvest of their labors.

We are grateful for the many who have joined the ranks of the few. We are grateful for all who have contributed to the spiritual climate of our larger community - for every hour spent; for every gift given; for every sacrifice made that moves our church nearer to your Kingdom on Earth.

As we worship and work together, O God:

- May our dreams flow from the fountain of all righteousness.
- May our goals be held in common.
- May every effort be offered in an attempt to do your holy will.

We affirm, O God, that our past is extremely memorable, but that our futures are far more exciting.

Enable us to be driven by your eternal purpose; motivated and empowered by your spirit; and may we be found faithful in all matters pertaining to your eternal kingdom.

Section Three

General Prayers

The Future is in Your Hands

Almighty God, whose presence is not contained within this vast universe but whose love can be experienced by the least and the last, we gather this day as your people to offer our praise and thanksgiving.

O God, we are often weak and defenseless. Certain temptations seem to override whatever will power we have. We allow so many petty annoyances to control us. We are held in bondage by our fears and hatreds. We cannot control our many appetites for the things of this world, and we have so little desire for the things of the Spirit.

We need your forgiveness and the assurance of your love and concern. Your words of Scripture come to us as a refreshing breeze, 'that as far as the East is from the West, so far you will remove our transgressions from us.'

Every time we worship, O God, we are confronted with new and fresh opportunities. Down deep in our soul we long for new beginnings. May this day surprise us with heavenly visions.

Today, O God, let each of us yield ourselves to you. May your will become our delight. May your way take control of our life. May your love become the pattern for all of our relationships.

So today, O God, we place into your caring hands, our families, immediate and extended, that joy may abound in our homes; our friends from our workplace and neighborhoods, that we may live peacefully together, and share our common troubles.

Enable us to know that our future is in your hands. May our choices be clear and our dedication be without reservation, as we seek to follow your Holy will. Grant to us a fresh assurance concerning your abiding love, and your grace without restriction.

Battle of Wills

Gracious Lord, for weeks now we have been asking ourselves the question, "What do You want to do through me?" Your Spirit reminds us that we are the People of God and because of that we are a people of prayer.

We realize, O God, that prayer at its best, is a dialogue with the Divine. We approach your throne in humility, asking that you would enable us to discern what your will is for our lives.

We confess, O God, that the battle of the wills is a powerful struggle going on within each one of us. We find ourselves on the verge of surrender to your will, then we back away hoping the spiritual urge will go away.

The conflict between mind and heart is a subtle but nagging controversy. Our heart suggests generosity, but our mind suggests that the heart is unreasonable. Our heart tends to think sacrificially, while our mind focuses on practicality.

But You, O God, can reveal to us the true measure of heart and mind, how both work together to make our faith complete. Enable us to realize that Christian commitment, is not about material goods over against spiritual values, it is about setting the proper priorities.

Your seed was planted in our hearts long ago, but we have not allowed it to take root and grow as it should. As a people struggling to become more mature, it is time to get everything right, and dedicate ourselves to your service with total mind and total heart.

May all those within our church family who are ill, be cured of their particular malady; may those who are carrying burdens too heavy, find their load lifted by a strong and purposeful God; and may our entire family share a common witness in support of those things that are in harmony with your Divine will.

Live Under God's Divine Leadership

O God, in whose image we are created, and who desires a strong bond with your creation. Make us aware that you are more to us than an ultimate vagueness or cosmic principle, you are one who knows and can be known.

Remind us, O God, that we are creatures with a beginning, but with an uncertain ending, for often our choices often override your prevailing will for our lives.

Help us to know that the only way we will ever be free from our own self domination, is to accept Christ as our Lord, and choose to live under his divine leadership.

We confess, O God, that the spiritual disciplines come difficult for us:

- In our worship we are often irreverent.
- In our study we are blatantly lazy.
- In our service we are grossly negligent.
- In our commitment we are timid and reluctant.

We spend our days building ant hills to no significant purpose. Your corrections are often painful, yet they come to us as blessings in disguise.

We long, O God, for a simple faith among life's complexities. So we ask:

- Give us the courage to face difficult days.
- Give us wisdom to make right choices.
- Give us the faith to accept your kingly rule.

Teach Us Values Worthy of This Hour

"**G**od of love and God of power, you have called us for this hour." We know, O God, that you have called us out of the world to be a chosen people, a royal priesthood, a holy nation, your own people.

Teach us the values of worship. May worship become the priority of our life. We often come seeking our own agenda, but let us meditatively listen for your agenda. As we wait in this holy place, let our spirits soar as eagles, lifting us above the chaos of our surroundings, yet keeping our feet on the ground, taking care of mundane matters as if they were holy.

Teach us the values of friendship. Some of our friends, O God, encourage us in matters of faith and loyalty, while others take lightly our Christian stewardship. Enable us to choose our friends carefully. Enable us to properly cultivate those who have like minds and like spirits, but to always practice kindness and hospitality to all those on a different journey.

Teach us the values needed as we relate to those in our workplace, as well as those who share our playground. May our knowledge and spiritual experience be sufficient for us to withstand the conflicts in our work and in our play. May our commitment remove the temptations of ever compromising our values. May our workplace reflect honor and dignity, and may our playgrounds re-create us for service in your eternal kingdom.

"God of love and God of power, make us worthy of this hour", but also worthy of the task which you have entrusted to each of us.

Spiritual Gifts

O God, who has endowed us with spiritual gifts and has therefore given us the ability to be his presence to others. Not all of us possess the same gifts, but we give you thanks for every gift entrusted to your children.

Your grace, O God, has come to us in so many ways and in so many places. Help us to realize that we praise your name the most is when we offer our individual gifts in the exercising of ministry.

Help us to discover our own unique giftedness. Help us to lay claim to those gifts you have so graciously given us. Help us to express each and every gift in this common task that is ours.

Let us never be jealous of the gifts other people bring to ministry, and let us not boast of our own gifts as if they were more important. Enable us to see the significance of all gifts-knowing that with each gift comes a corresponding responsibility.

Let the harmony of our many gifts provide sweet music to our Father's ears.

Be our inward strength, that we may be strong for outward responsibilities.

Bless the sick, the bereaved and the lonely.

Set our hearts on things above that we might reflect your love in our many enterprises here on earth.

Personal Responsibility

Almighty and Everlasting God, creator of this vast universe, yet the giver of each individual gift. We pause before your throne of grace, realizing that we, too often, call upon you with words neatly chosen, but with hearts greatly removed.

In days of old, O God, whenever the people desired to be in your presence, smoke would descend on the holy mountain. The prophet would receive your message and communicate it to the people. We gather this day before your holy altar and await some word that will lift our spirits, increase our faith and deepen our commitment.

- We realize, O God, to worship a powerful God, is to reap a powerful fellowship.
- To worship a God of love, is to reap a community of people who are willing to share their love with us freely and openly.
- To worship a generous God, is to reap a community of people who have developed generous hearts and systematic patterns of giving.

You have been so good to us, O God. You have blessed us with greater numbers and remarkable achievements. You have given us a powerful vision, with the talents and gifts to make it a reality. May each of us accept the personal responsibility to accept a full share in the work and ministry of your Church.

True Discipleship

O God, you have called us into a priesthood of believers; you have nurtured us through Scripture, prayer and regular worship; and, you have destinations for us to reach far beyond our imagination. We sense that we are on the threshold of becoming an obedient church. All that is required of us is the will to be faithful.

You have planted the seed of faith within us, and we have felt it grow gradually, but surely, until now it seeks to blossom forth in true discipleship.

We realize that our minds and hearts are too small and fickle to accommodate the vastness of your dreams. We ask that you expand our minds and enlarge our hearts. Make our hearts your dwelling place, and may our actions be true movements of your Spirit. Make us:

- Pure without corruption.
- Sober without dullness.
- And true without duplicity.

May our doubts lead us into greater knowledge, and may our suffering, from whatever experience, be a catalyst that deepens and sweetens our faith.

Let us never be content with our imperfections. Engage us in your work that challenges our minds and quickens our spirits.

May this day become Day 1 in our spiritual renewal. Let us take seriously the responsibilities of discipleship. Where we have wasted our time and talents, let us accept new opportunities that match our spiritual gifts.

Bring us to the place in ministry where commitment is not a burden, but a joy.

God's Power Through Repentance

O God, whose love is most clearly defined in the life and ministry of Jesus Christ, inspire us through the indwelling of your Holy Spirit, so that our greatest desire would be to become perfect in love.

Like the prophet Isaiah, when we experience your holiness, we realize our own sinfulness. In our more truthful moments, we realize that we are persons of unclean lips, who dwell among a people of unclean lips. Our hearts are divided. Our soul sees through two eyes. Our tongue confesses one Lord, but our life reflects many.

Save us from evasions and deceits of a soft complacency with which we excuse ourselves. For all that has been wrong in us, O God, we earnestly strive to repent and amend our ways. So we bring our:

- Sins to be forgiven.
- Fears to be dispelled.
- Anxieties to be overcome.
- Discouragements to be driven out.

Make us adequate for life's encounters. Give us the strength to face life as it really is, the courage to face ourselves, and the spirit and sense of devotion to seek avenues of new experiences in your love. Where we have once witnessed weakness, may we now witness power. Where we have once witnessed complacency, may we now witness a refreshing enthusiasm of spirit.

You know our needs, O God, even before we ask, but in simple trust of your forgiving, healing and restoring power, we place our needs before you with the assurance of your divine response.

Let the Spirit Help Us Rise Above Our Ordinary Self

Creator of the earth and skies, to whom all truth and power belong. Grant us your truth to make us wise. Grant us your power to make us strong.

How perfect are your ways, O God, and how polluted and distorted are ours. We find ourselves at the center of conflict, without and within.

- Our world is torn apart by international conflict.
- There is conflict in our work place, where jealousy rules over position, salary and benefits.
- Our marriages are troubled, often beyond repair.
- We are constantly torn between Your praises and self-adulation.
- We have made promises we have not kept, and we no long feel guilty about them.
- Even we, ourselves, have grown weary with our petty problems, and our resistance to divine guidance.

Many of our sins are quietly smoldering just beneath the façade of our outward witness. The choice is ours, either to fan them into flame, or to turn them over to you to be forgiven and removed.

You, O God, are the source of true holiness, and only you can bring our conflicted lives into harmony with your divine will.

Grant us the will and the power, through your Holy Spirit, to rise above our ordinary self, where ego rules and greed dominates, to that place where all is redeemed and you are in absolute control of our lives.

God of Healing and Hope

God of healing and God of hope, we bring our brokenness and our disillusionments before your gracious throne, knowing that it is your nature to heal, and to instill hope in the hearts of your children.

There is so much in us, O God that needs healing.

- Our bodies suffer all kinds of ailments that medicine doesn't seem to cure.
- Our minds are fragmented with too many thoughts that have little merit.
- Our spirits are downcast because so many of our relationships are fruitless – and our own self-image distorts your creation.

We are healed by love.

- Show us the love that sustains our weakness.
- Show us the love that enlightens our darkness.
- Show us the love that mends our brokenness and reconciles our alienation.

We need more than healing, O God, we need to be hopeful as well. How can we be hopeful in an insecure and often violent world?

- Economic uncertainties abound.
- War looms on the horizon.
- There is danger at every turn.

We realize, O God, in you alone is our hope!

- Where humanity fails – you succeed.
- We have tried our way – now give us the faith and courage to try things your way.
- God make us hopeful!

Give us hope:

- Reconciliation can come out of conflict.
- Peace can be found between bitter enemies.
- Cures can be found for debilitating diseases.
- Sorrow can be turned into joy.
- And that out of death comes resurrection.

Let us go forth from this place healed from all of our maladies and with hopeful hearts to face the great unknown.

Penitent Confession and Life Giving Forgiveness

O God, who surely grieves over a broken and bleeding world, for this moment in time, we open our hearts and lift our voices, in praise and thanksgiving to you, who can bring all factions together and make everything right.

In order to right our wrongs, we need to spiritually prostrate ourselves, before your throne, in humble confession. Hear our confession, O God.

- That we often speak before we think.
- That we walk too close to temptation.
- For not doing those things we intended to do, because we lacked the will to do it.
- For our impatience.
- For coveting those things that belong to someone else.
- For cultivating bad habits instead of weeding them out.
- For finding fault with others, without prior self-examination.
- For being too interested in peripheral matters while ignoring the essential.

Remove from us, O God, the temptations that attract and hold our attention – and remove the sins which have stained our lives.

As a forgiven people, O God, grant us your blessing:

- Bless our families and those close to us that love would be the rule in our life and harmony would prevail.
- Bless those who are experiencing any kind of illness, especially those who have been diagnosed with conditions for which there is no known cure.
- Bless all of us who are bound by chains of any kind that are too strong for us to cast off.
- Bless each one of us individually – and minister to the private concerns of every heart.

Give to each of us a spirit that truly desires to live a good and godly life.

Give to each of us a desire to acquire the gifts of the spirit.
Give to each of us more control over our life, where our old nature is discarded and our new nature acquired.

God of Love and God of Power

"**G**od of Love and God of Power – thou hast called us for this hour." The words of this refrain, O God, stirs our hearts and challenges our minds. Love is the essence of our existence. Without love we are a noisy gong or clanging cymbal.

It is by your Love, O God, we have:

- Light for our darkness.
- Courage for our fears.
- Hope for our despair.
- Peace for our turmoil.
- Joy for our sorrow.
- Wisdom for our confusion.
- Humility for our arrogance.
- And tenderness for our toughness.

Your love, O God, molds our character and shapes our witness.

But we realize, O God, that love without power is to possess your divine nature, but without strength or ability to express it. So we pray, O God, for power!

- We need your power that enables us to speak with authority to proclaim your divine goodness.
- We need your power to transcend the ordinary.
- We need your power to turn our no's into yes's.
- We need your power to turn our timidity into boldness.
- We need your power to move us to a higher level of under-standing and commitment.
- We need your power to transform our faltering faith into a dy-namic and courageous expression of your redeeming love.

"God of Love and God of Power – thou hast called us for this hour!" Not tomorrow – not next week – but today – this moment. Grant to us, O God, these qualities now that will reshape and rekindle our lives for tomorrow and for eternity Bless all of us who have special concerns this morning. May we find strength and consolation in your presence – may our needs be met – and may we go forth to live as those who bear witness to your refining love.

Our Body, Your Will

O God, your word reveals that you are Spirit, and if we are to worship, we must do so in spirit and in truth.

You have created us from the dust of the earth, yet our essential being is spiritual, not physical. Being created in your likeness, our primary motivation is internal, not external. Even though we are created with physical extremities, we are directed by the Spirit.

We realize, O God that you have no hands but ours. May our hands be regularly folded in prayer; may they be outstretched to welcome the stranger; and may they be put to the plow, never to look back.

We realize, O God, that you have no feet but ours. May we always walk the proper path; and may our feet lead us to destinations of your choosing.

We realize, O God, that you have no arms but ours. Let us embrace each other and the children of the world with love that knows no limits.

We realize, O God, that you have no eyes but ours. Let us see clearly the work you have entrusted to us; and may you keep a vision of the cross before us as we seek to do your will.

We realize, O God, that you have no ears but ours. Make us sensitive to the sound of your voice as well as the cries of the world.

Make us aware, O God, that there is no other vehicle through which your work is carried out other than through the Body of Christ, Your church.

May we be alert and responsive to the call and needs of our day.

Special Grace

O God, whose nature is love and whose will is ever directed to your children's good. We approach your hallowed throne this day grateful for your divine presence that guides our steps, yet confessing how often we seek to follow our own way and will.

- How often we experience the ambivalence of faithfulness and faithlessness.
- How often our words are in conflict with our life.
- How often we intend to please you with our actions, yet our good intentions lead to divine disappointment.
- How many times we have made positive resolutions, yet have fallen back into old patterns.

We know that out of love you are willing to forgive us, if we will but ask and accept your gracious pardon.

We pray for your special grace in this hour, not for the sake of the moment, but that all of our lives be elevated and strengthened that we may live in your world as witnesses to your saving grace and overwhelming love.

May your presence in our life and your influence in our life be so real to us that we may never again lose sight of your purpose for our life. May:

- Our family life be more wholesome.
- Our friendships more faithful.
- Our difficulties borne with greater fortitude.
- Our bereavements endured with greater peace.
- And our common work be done with an uncommon fidelity.

In Christ's Name.

(Also available on audio- "Prayers for Daily Living"- Track 22)

Bless Godly Institutions and Leaders

O God, who dwells in high places – we lift our hearts and voices in praise and thanksgiving. We confess, O God, that our thoughts are not your thoughts – and neither are our ways your ways.

For much of our life we have traveled the low road, the road of self-satisfaction. We have followed one path of least resistance. Only when your Spirit mingles with our spirit does our earthly fixation entertain heavenly possibilities.

When we are in your presence – you are constantly calling us to:

- Elevate our thinking.
- Purify our hearts.
- Cleanse ourselves of our habits.
- Walk the road less traveled.

Enable us to abandon all thoughts and ways that are contrary to your holy will.

We are grateful for all institutions that witness to your divine love. We pray for our church – not a product of human hands – but a fellowship created by your divine initiative.

We know, O God, that our purpose is singular – to spread the gospel of holiness throughout the earth. Encourage our discipleship and empower us to be faithful witnesses.

We are also grateful for every human institution that builds character and promotes goodness. We are grateful for every mature and dedicated leader whose teachings are harmonious with your nature, and whose lives are exemplary. We are grateful for boys and girls whose intuition is to follow the precepts and examples of those who lead them.

We pray this day for every sort and condition of persons:

- Bless those who have recently lost a loved one. May their memory remain to inspire us and encourage us.
- Bless those who are ill or undergoing tests of any kind. May a diagnosis be made quickly and a cure to follow.
- Bless all of us who have troubled hearts. May your hand of comfort make easier our days.

Enable Us to Hear Your Voice

Eternal God, whose purpose and whose laws pervade this vast universe and makes of it one world – we offer our praise and thanksgiving.

We know, O God, much of our devotion is directed toward false gods and petty ideals – when we need to direct our lives in a single direction toward your goodness and love. Save us from cynicism and skepticism – from all maladies of mind and spirit that would spoil our lives and damage our witness.

Grant to us a full measure of faith we would accept and promote the values that are beautiful and good. May our lives be drawn to your values that are consistent with your nature and will.

When many voices are clamoring for our attention, enable us to hear your voice, clear and unmistakable, calling us to ultimate loyalty.

Enable us to hear above all others:

- The voice of truth that denies all falsehood.
- The voice of righteousness that shuns all evil.
- The voice of love that call us from fear and hatred.

We pray for all sorts and conditions of persons:

- For those who have suffered the loss of a family member or friend – be our strong comfort.
- For those whose health needs a caring and healing hand.
- For those who suffer from any affliction of body, mind or spirit – may your presence lift them from despair and hope.

We offer this prayer.

Cultivate in Us the Holy Habit of Worship

Almighty and Eternal God, creator of the vast universe, yet the creator of each individual life. We pause before your gracious throne, surrounded by mysteries too great for us to comprehend, yet worshipping a God who has revealed himself in the life, death, and resurrection of our Lord.

We are reminded that one custom of Jesus was to be in the synagogue every Sabbath. Cultivate in us this holy habit that nourishes our soul and energizes our witness. May this time of worship be, for us, a time of spiritual renewal. A time for us to claim our roots and reaffirm our baptism.

May we be willing to give up those things that prevent us from being a faithful disciple. May you reward us with your guiding and sustaining Spirit.

May we feel this morning the strong beat of your divine heart, moving and stirring our reluctant souls. May those of us who have been smoldering ashes, burst out into a burning flame. May our spirit of rededication be rekindled throughout this congregation and beyond.

Our petitions this morning, O God, are:

- Show compassion upon those who need a gentle and gracious encounter.
- Give strength to those whose footsteps have faltered and who need to be lifted up out of their despair and weakness.
- Give comfort to those who have experienced great sadness that they might know the joy that comes from your divine ministry.

Make us captives of your Spirit, Lord, for only then will we know what it truly means to be free.

Life is Good

O God, by your good grace, we receive the marvelous gifts of life. Your delight is in sharing your love and generosity with us. We affirm the goodness of all created things.

- We affirm that life is good because we share your Spirit of freedom and love.
- Work is good when our gifts are employed constructively.
- Marriage is good when we share our life with someone who returns our love and shares our sorrow.
- Children are good for you have made us co-creators with you. What pleasure you have and we ourselves have when our children strive for spiritual fulfillment.
- Fellowship is good when we can witness to our faith among those who share our joy.

We remember that Jesus said: "You shall know the truth and the truth shall make you free."

- Free us from those things that seek to imprison us.
- Free us from our selfish desire.
- Free us from false and petty ideals.
- Free us from doubts and disillusionments.

Make us free to share our love in bountiful proportions. Let us never think that all our material goods are strictly ours to keep and to use – But that all of our resources come from you – and that we have the pleasure of both receiving and giving through channels of love that enriches community and world.

You have blessed this congregation so richly. May we have the depth of faith to offer it back generously.

You know the needs of all of us – so minister to us that we might find health, peace, comfort, and hope. This prayer we offer in the same of Jesus.

God of Our Senses and Mind

O God, who dwells in places light years away – yet who is as close to us as we choose you to be – offer to us this day some fresh revelation of the nature of your character.

Open our eyes that we may see the wonder of your world – that we may proclaim the beauty of your creation. You have so created us that we are able to see:

- The majestic sunrise and beautiful sunset.
- The mountain ranges capped with snow.
- The breaking of the surf.
- The smile of a little child.

Open our ears that we may hear the sound of your voice that comes to us in many ways:

- The song of the bird.
- The wind thru the trees.
- The words of those who express their love to us.
- Sounds that proclaim your power - but also sounds that express the sweetness of your love.

Open our minds through the revelation of new truths:

- May the knowledge we receive enable us to clarify our faith position.
- May our knowledge, gained by study, and empowered by prayer, simply reveal the wisdom of one who has created all things and who seeks for us to live in harmony with all your creatures.

Open our lips that we may extol your greatness.

- That we may speak of your gracious acts.
- May the student in us become the teacher as we share with our children, family and friends the story of a God, so powerful and loving, that he was willing to go to the cross to prove it.

As the sights, sounds and knowledge of your love come to us thru our senses:

- May be respond with a faith that is vital and urgent.
- A faith that transforms and sustains.
- A faith that brings healing and wholeness to our life and witness.
- A faith that overcomes all doubt and weakness.

A Prayer of Confession and Refreshing

O God, who knows our every mood, you hear our shouts of joy as well as our cries of anguish. You celebrate with us in our victories and you console us in our defeats. You strengthen us in our weakness and humble us in our successes.

We confess, O God, at times your work is our delight – while at other times it conflicts with our own self interests. Enable us to lay all of our sin before you – sins of the past and sins of the present – sins that we try to hide – and those that we seem to boast and brag about.

- Forgive us when we shirk our responsibilities.
- Forgive us for being proud of our own opinions while discounting the opinions of others.
- Forgive us for seeing the impediment in our neighbor's eye while ignoring an even larger impediment in our own eye.

Let us receive and cherish your response to our confession – hearing the words: "Your sins are forgiven!"

We have chosen, O God, to worship you this day for some reason perhaps not clear to us, but make us glad we came.

While we are in your holy presence:

- Refresh our minds that we may think thoughts that are good and wholesome.
- Refresh our bodies with new strength and energy.
- Refresh our spirits with a power that deepens our commitment and strengthens our will to be faithful.

We ask, O God, that you may deepen our sense of caring for friend and foe alike. Enable us to be an advocate for the poor and those who have no voice in public matters. Be to each one of us exactly what we need, that our faith will be strong and our witness genuine.

Confession Good for the Soul

O God, whose light encircles our universe – whose truth dispels every doubt – and whose love embraces all humankind – we gather once more in your presence to offer our praise and thanksgiving.

In the presence of your glory it is easy to see our own shortcomings. We confess that:

- Our eyes have become accustomed to the things of this world.
- We have become desensitized to those things that are contrary to your will.
- We too often lift up our modern culture as the standard of moral conduct.
- We suffer the rapids and whirlpools of our daily existence as if life were meant to be that way.

We know, O God, confession is good for the soul and that forgiveness is our cherished desire.

Remind us, O God, of the goodness that surrounds us – of the beauty you have set before us – and the friendships that make positive contributions to our life.

We pray this day:

- For the light to walk by.
- For the strength to persevere.
- For the comfort that eases our hurt.
- For the love that enables us to embrace friend and enemy alike.

Remind us that we will not leave this place dependent upon our own resources, but your power makes all things possible.

Hear the unspoken prayers that rise in silence from the depths of our hearts; and minister to each of us according to the riches of your grace in Christ Jesus.

Enable Us to Realize Our Spiritual Potential

Eternal God, who understands the mysteries of the universe, yet who understands the minutest concerns of the human heart and mind, we praise you with our lips and worship you from the depths of our hearts.

Enable us, O God, to see ourselves as you see us!

- As children created in your spiritual likeness.
- As part of your creation whom you have called "good", and to whom you have entrusted the care of all living things.
- What a high and holy status you have given us.

You are aware, O God, of our every character flaw, yet you accept us and claim us as your very own. You know our thoughts and intentions. You have given us the freedom to be disobedient, yet you continue to lovingly nurture us back to obedience. Help us to claim our God-given worth.

Enable us, God, to realize our spiritual potential.

You provide us with worship that is both exciting and relevant, yet it is often low among our priorities. You offer us resources for our spiritual development, yet they are systematically ignored.

The gift of time is a precious commodity, yet we let so much of it slip away frivolously. You have shown us what is important, yet we focus on the trivial. Your light has brilliantly lighted our path, yet we have chosen to live in the shadows.

Show us, once again, O God, we can become Christ-like to each other.

Be with all of us this day who are struggling with hurts that won't heal, with sorrow that is inconsolable, and with disappointments that drag us down into despair. Set our feet on right paths; fill our minds with holy thoughts; and may our lives be true witnesses to your love.

(Also available on audio- "Prayers for Daily Living"- Track 12)

God, Open Our Senses to Your Will

God of wisdom, power, and pure goodness, we come before your throne of grace with lives that are unclean, but with hearts desiring spiritual purification.

You have given us the remarkable gift of using our senses in order to experience, understand and appreciate the wonders of your creation.

Open our eyes that we may be able to see the spiritual deprivation that haunts our world, as well as our own limitations and shortcomings. May we be able to see your goodness through all those whom we encounter.

Open our ears that we may be able to hear the cries of those who are hungry, lonely, sick, and imprisoned. May their suffering catch and hold our attention until we are compelled to respond.

Open our mouths that we may first proclaim your gospel message to those in this part of your world, and then may we speak words of kindness and love to our friends, neighbors, and strangers alike.

Open our hands that we may serve your holy will with strength and gladness. May the things that we hold on to be the things of the Spirit.

Direct our steps as we seek to walk in your way. May the path of the cross be the path we have chosen. So guide us to the road less traveled.

Open wide the doors of our hearts that we will not only receive your generosity but that we shall also offer gracious hospitality to those around us.

You have said to us "Knock and it will be opened; seek and we will find; ask and it will be given." O God, you know our needs before we ask. As each one of us waits in your presence just now, we beseech you to respond to our deepest and innermost needs. May we be able to leave this place with hearts that are free and spirits that overflow with your love.

(Also available on audio- "Prayers for Daily Living"- Track 10)

Worshipping God Alone Enables Us

In the words of the Psalmist, we lift our voices in affirmation, "I lift up my eyes to the hills from whence does my help come, my help comes from the Lord, who made heaven and earth."

We confess that in our culture there are so many things that claim our attention. We have a way of chasing false gods. The secular attractions of wealth, pleasure and prestige seem to promise so much, yet when we have them alone our lives are hollow and unfulfilled.

It is our affirmation that there is no god but the God of Abraham, Isaac, and Jacob – The God of Grace revealed in Jesus of Nazareth. There is no intelligence outside of your wisdom. There is no power outside your mighty hand. You have no rivals, O God, only false hopes fueled by our own selfishness.

Enable us, O God, to know the truth.

Enable us, O God, to feel your presence.

Enable us, O God, to be energized by your power.

We as a congregation, O God, have entered into a Holy Covenant:

- To live and work in the spirit of unity.
- To bring our will into submission with your will.
- To seek nothing except your love and peace.

May our focus be singular and our intentions pure; where there is discord among us, replace it with spiritual harmony.

There are strong needs among our people. There is illness, loneliness, disappointment. Whatever our need, we are confident that we will find our help in you.

Give Us a Fresh Desire to Follow You

Almighty God, who spoke and the world began, and who continues to speak either thru ways few understand, or by a still small voice that gives us comfort and encouragement. We gather this day to offer our praise and adoration.

The created world, O God, reflects your glory, both in design and dependability. How wonderfully and beautifully everything is made. Everything works together in marvelous harmony. Enable us to catch a glimpse of your divine plan for your world as well as through our lives.

Over against your majesty we realize our own human predicament – how our own disobedience has placed the desires of self above your desires. We confess that our own will is bent toward serving our own perceived needs. We are examples of intentions gone wrong – of decisions aborted and goals unfulfilled. Yet your word reminds us "if we confess our sins you are faithful and just to forgive our sins and will cleanse us from all unrighteousness."

May this day bring to us a new and fresh desire to follow your way and will. We know we cannot live by bread alone. May we recapture that special vision that enables us to see ourselves as you see us. By your grace transform us into:

- Agents of reconciliation.
- Vessels of service.
- Obedient children.

We come, O God, with a multitude of needs:

- Some of us are facing the dilemma of old age.
- Some of us are young – needing discipline for our unbridled enthusiasm.
- Some of us are ill.

- Some are bereaved.
- Some of us are indecisive and uncertain.

All of us need the spiritual resources. Be to each of us what we sorely need this day.

(Also available on audio- "Prayers for Daily Living"- Track 21)

Come Close to Us, O God

O God, whose light overcomes our darkness; whose truth enlightens our minds; and whose love satisfies the longings of our heart. We gather this day to offer our praise and thanksgiving and to seek your divine help.

Come close to each of us in our personal troubles:

- Some of us have felt the pain of recent losses and have felt the disappointments of our neighbors.
- Some of us are facing tough decisions that are difficult to understand and manage.
- Some of us are separated or estranged from members of our own family and our heart aches with loneliness.
- Some of us have made bad decisions and we are suffering the consequences.
- Some of us are facing uncertain times and are anxious concerning our future.
- Some of us are trapped in our own self-centered world and cannot see beyond our own walls.

O God, there are so many problems and so few self-sought answers.

- We lift our eyes heavenward.
- We lay bare our heart and soul.
- We long for and need your divine visitation and help.

We need more than our own resources will provide.

- We need your mighty wisdom and your powerful leadership.
- We need to feel the comfort of our enduring presence.

- We need to experience the healing that comes from your personal touch.
- We need to be guided on to right paths and strengthened in all of our enduring relationships.

Be to us, O God, whatever we need and let us feel the assurance of your everlasting love.

We Bring Our Total Selves to You

Almighty God, who has created us in your own image, you have given us the power to reason and the capacity to love each other. You have given us the capability of doing magnificent things. The symphony of our own system amazes even us. In our high spiritual moments we recall the words of the apostle Paul – that we should present our bodies as a living sacrifice, holy and acceptable to you.

O God, we are tired of fighting battles that we cannot win. The ways of the world are too much for us. We are overwhelmed with our passion for things. The noises of the street drown out the whispers of our heart.

So, we bring to you the totality of our being:

- Help us to pray today with our minds – as we lift our thoughts heavenward.
- Help us to pray with our eyes – looking and searching for your hidden treasures.
- Help us to pray with our ears as we listen for that still small voice; and enable us to hear the cries of anguish from our fellow human beings.
- Help us to pray with our hands as we raise them in joyful praise and as we seek to lift the burden from our neighbor's shoulders.
- Help us to pray with our feet as we walk the via dolorosa; and as we stop lightly in the fear of offending our neighbor
- Help us to pray with our heart – filled with the noises of our own choosing. May the secular voices be silenced in us as we worship the One who continues to speak that authentic word.

May the One who stilled the winds and the waves still the restlessness of our heart, and bring peace to our inner being.

In this moment of contrition, O God, we bring all that we are and all that we have into your presence in an attempt at renewal – seeking to commit ourselves to your will and way.

Here Am I Lord, Send Me!

Almighty God, whose light never fades and whose love never fails, we gather in this sacred place this morning to worship you in spirit and in truth. In this divine encounter, O God, we know that you are forever faithful and we are always less than you expect us to be.

We realize that our thoughts only touch the outskirts of your way and our imaginations are but partial pictures of your truth. Our thoughts are not your thoughts; neither are our ways your ways.

We come to you because you are the only one who can cleanse our hearts and remold our minds.

When we are honest with ourselves, we realize that we are self-serving and apathetic toward spiritual values. We are guilty of trying to manipulate others for our own gain. We are constantly scheming to take advantage of someone else's weakness.

Look deep into our hearts and purify our motives and forgive us for our spiritual disobedience.

- Forgive us for hearing your word and not following it.
- Forgive us for knowing your word and not loving it.
- Forgive us for confessing to believe your word and not living it.

Today is a new day in our life. Enable us to take on new challenges and opportunities. You know our gifts are diverse but many. Show us the ways we can more faithfully serve.

May this be the day that we say "yes" to your call. There are jobs to be done and tasks to be completed. May our faith be demonstrated in multiple ways.

Give us a passion for service! You have said that "the harvest is plentiful, but the laborers are few." Give us the insight to realize how our particular gifts can be enlisted in your service and grant us one measure of conviction and courage of faith to say "Here am I Lord, send me!"

Take Control of Our Lives and Of Your World

"O God, of every nation, of every race and land,
Redeem your whole creation with your almighty hand.
Where hate and fear divide us and bitter threats are hurled,
In love and mercy guide us and heal our strife-torn world."

These words from your poet mirror the hopes and dreams of us all. We find ourselves wandering in the wilderness of our own self-centeredness, indecision and apathy. In these uncertain times we long for that which is stable and certain.

- In a world where doubt dominates our hearts and minds – reveal to us the truth of the ages.
- In a world where hatred seems to triumph – replace our partisan jealousy with your redeeming love.
- In a world where conflict exposes our selfish interests – let the idea of peace take root in our hearts.
- In a world where faith is expressed in many different ways – may all of us realize the source of your amazing grace.
- In a world where there is blatant disregard for each other – enable us to reaffirm that all of us are created in your image.
- In a world where the light of freedom seems to flicker and possibly go out – enable us to remember that all of the darkness of this world cannot extinguish even one small candle.

O God, when our times seem the more perilous, we feel your nearness the most. We have felt your presence as we have stood shoulder to shoulder praying for your protection and guidance.

We have felt the Spirit move within us as we have pledged our loyalty to our nation and to our God. Our hearts have overflowed as we have sung the stirring songs of our faith Take control of our lives and of your world. May your purposes be clear and your love explicit as we commit ourselves to do your holy will.

(Also available on audio- "Prayers for Daily Living"- Track 8)

Here We Are Lord, Use Us!

Eternal God, we gather in your house with regularity to hear what you have to say.

- We are moved by your Scripture.
- We are enlightened by your interpreters.
- We are enriched by the music that affirms and praises your name.
- We are filled with joy as we embrace each other in this sacred fellowship.

But we know, O God, there are times you need to hear from us. Your word is so explicit and challenging. What we hear you saying is:

- Whom shall I send?
- Who will go for me?
- Who will share their life sacrificially?

Give wisdom to our response and an enduring strength to our commitment!

You have given us gifts, not simply for us to enjoy but to use them to glorify your name.

- If our gift is teaching – let us drink long at the fountain of knowledge – both biblical and secular, that we may offer a faithful and inspired witness.
- If our gift is music – let the melody of our hearts be expressed through the words and sounds we offer up!
- If our gift is time – let us be systematic and generous.
- If our gift is caring – let us do so with love, patience and deep compassion.
- If our gift is of monetary value – let it be shared in the same spirit in which it has been received. Do not let our possessions

possess us. But, under the guidance of your Spirit, let us offer an exemplary stewardship.

May your people gathered here offer a unified voice as we say: "Here we are Lord, send us!" "Here we are Lord, use us!" "Let our gifts be matched with our devotion!

God, Give Us the Desires of Our Hearts

O God, to whom every spirit bears witness, we acknowledge your love for us that comes in so many wonderful and mysterious ways.

We confess, O God, that the tragedy of our humanity is that we experience love on different levels. On one level we experience a perverted self-love that overflows its natural boundaries in our selfish pursuit of worldly pleasures. We tend to love ourselves with a non-spiritual love that rewards itself in the acquisition and pleasures of earthly toys.

At the same time, O God, we are seeking a love on a deeper level. A love that recognizes the divine within, and desires to be in union with your love. A love that causes our hearts to overflow with goodness and joy.

We confess too, O God, we tend to love you for what you can do for us. Even in our selfish pursuits your goodness and mercy is experienced in abundance. We realize you love us on a level far beyond our comprehension with a love that we do not deserve or appreciate. Even when we ask for worldly goods you reward us with spiritual blessing.

We turn to you in the storms of life, and we feel that your presence quiets the waves and hushes the winds. Help us, O God, to continually reach higher for that love that is infinitely sweeter and far more rewarding.

Enable us, O God, to reach that level of love, where your mind becomes our mind; where your will becomes our will; and where the desires of your heart kindles the flame of desire in our hearts.

God, Make Us Aware Of What We Have to Contribute

O God, the giver of every perfect gift and before whom we stand accountable for our actions. We pause before your gracious throne humbly pleading our own case.

As the Psalmist wrote, "we acknowledge our transgressions and our sin is ever before us." We realize that we bring nothing into the world and can take nothing out; and all the while we are here, we have no merit to warrant your free grace. We come before you in faith alone believing if we come in true repentance, forgiveness will be granted.

As we wait in your presence, as forgiven sinners, make us aware of the things in our life that we can contribute regardless how meager our existence; how unassuming our talent; each of us have personal contributions we can make. To have something to contribute and fail to do so, may be the worst sin of all.

- Each of us possesses a certain knowledge that no one else possesses – may we use what we have in witnessing to the truth.
- Each of us possesses certain gifts that are unique to our own personality – may we be able to express them to enrich others.
- We possess the same amount of time – may we preserve enough of it that we can devote a significant share to serving the needs of others.

Give us a sense of satisfaction in accomplishment, and a greater sense of guilt in neglect. Give us pride in our work, but humbleness in its approach.

- For things done – give us the pleasure of sharing it.
- For things undone – may we find a fresh desire to do it.

Speak to every heart in this place this morning and may the response you receive be the response you desire.

My Our Response Match Your Expectations

Eternal God, Father of us all, we gather in your holy presence to avail ourselves of your wisdom, power, and strength. You are merciful beyond our imagination and loving beyond our comprehension. We stand in awe of your magnificent love.

We ask, O God, that you come to each of us in these moments of intimacy to understand our struggle and to have mercy upon our selfish ways. We confess that we are a people preoccupied with our selfish desires.

- We cannot help being worried.
- We have quarreled with those close to us.
- We have been negligent concerning the needs of our neighbors.
- We worry about stretching our money in order to meet all of our worldly obligations.
- There are questions about our health that dominates our minds.

All of these things are important to us right now! You have taught us to bring everything to you in prayer. Here they are Lord. Enable us to leave them with you and find some relief from our anxieties.

Hear always, O God, our prayers of intercession.

- We pray for those in our church family who have become distracted from their spiritual journey.
- We pray for those who have fallen upon hard times.
- We pray for those who suffer the consequences of wrong choices.
- We pray for those who suffer illness or loss within and without our circle of caring.

We pray for our church, your church, as it seeks to provide a faithful and generous witness. We pray that our commitment will exceed the challenge. That the gifts we offer will more than satisfy the needs. May our commitment be a definitive statement of our ever growing and developing faith.

O God, we acknowledge that you have given us so much. May our response match your expectations.

Begin Each Day with a Grateful Heart

O God, we affirm the words of your Psalmist when he wrote: "The Lord is my Shepherd, I lack for nothing!" We have witnessed your goodness at every turn. You have supplied our every need even though we have an insatiable appetite for more and more.

We are a people who have received bountiful portions of everything, but we have failed to live the abundant life.

- We are blessed with food sources beyond our expectation – both healthy and indulgent.
- We are blessed with extravagant shelters of all shapes and sizes.
- You have ordained marriage by giving us a soul mate who satisfies our longings for intimacy.
- You have blessed us with the gift of children.
- You have made available to us, at our own choosing, our most meaningful relationships.
- We are free to worship as we choose – or whether we choose.
- Our basic civil rights are guarded by our constitution you planted in the minds of our fore parents!

Help us to begin each day with an attitude that comes from a grateful heart.

- Keep us strong that we may help the weak.
- Keep us free that we may help to secure freedom for those in bondage.
- Keep us faithful that we may be the light to other nations.
- Keep our love for the truth so intense that we may enlighten those who follow false gods.

Let us not be intimidated by threats. Enable us to be cautious, not careless. Enable us to practice a vigilance that gives us confidence in today and hope for tomorrow.

Teach us that there is no condition or situation that cannot be resolved if we will but trust in your divine judgment and leadership.

Make Us Strong! Make Us Diligent!

Eternal God, your word teaches us that you are the same yesterday – today – and tomorrow. When we are ambivalent in our beliefs and actions, we can be sure that your nature never changes.

We come into your presence for different reasons:

- There are times when we are almost pure in thought and simply want to be near you.
- There are times we are selfish, seeking personal favors.
- There are times that the world is too much with us and we need relief.

With whatever spirit we approach your throne, we know that we will be heard and our situations resolved. In matters of faith – make us strong! In matters of service – keep us diligent!

- When we are slow to choose the right way, be patient with us and guide our steps to right paths.
- When we are disillusioned, lead us through our doubts and enable us to embrace the truth.
- When we are reluctant witnesses, make us more decisive.

As a congregation, O God:

- Soften our sadness and spark our enthusiasm.
- Lift our hopes and heal our hurts.
- Reconcile us in our relationships and feed our souls with the bread of righteousness.

O God, we have concerns on our hearts that are too heavy for our fragile bodies and spirits.

- Some of our faith family suffer from maladies of body, mind or spirit. Heal us!
- Some of our families have felt the devastating loss of precious family members or friends. Console us!
- Some of our families are living on the edge and are anxious about the future. Strengthen us and give us hope!

We have discovered there are many ways to suffer, O God, but you know them all. Minister to us where we are – with what we need – that we may leave this place with hearts that are lighter and our spirits lifted to new heights.

Restore Us to Right Living

Eternal God, who watches over us with a sleepless vigil, we praise your holy name in thought, word and music.

We realize, O God, we are not here by chance, but by divine choice. You have formed us and made us the persons we are – You compare us with no other.

You created us with free will. We can either go right or wrong. We are free to obey your calling, which brings ultimate fulfillment, or we are free to disobey, which leads us into a life of chaos and ruin.

- When our lives go wrong, we drift away from you, and lose our connection.
- When our lives go wrong, our will collides with your will, and we are at odds with the world.
- When our lives go wrong there is discord in the home.
- When our lives go wrong, our friendships turn sour.
- When our lives go wrong, our perverted journey takes us into the far country.

We affirm, O God, nothing good happens when our lives go wrong! But Thou, O God, are One who makes all things right.

- When our lives are right, the distance between us disappears.
- When our lives are right, we see glorious new beginnings and possibilities.
- When our lives are right, we see others as extensions of your creation.
- When our lives are right, there is no mountain too high that we cannot climb, or valley too deep that we cannot endure.

- When our lives are right, O God, we find joy in every encounter, and hope in every difficulty.

(Also available on audio- "Prayers for Daily Living"- Track 27)

Enable Us to Build Our Life Around Values That Endure

Our Father God, whose handiwork reveals the measure of your mind and whose gift of Christ reveals the depth of your love. In faith we come this morning, strong in the belief that you have done for us far more than we can think or imagine.

We give thanks this day for all people great and good who have strived to remain faithful to the Christian witness – who have sought to be a good neighbor – and who carefully and lovingly nurture their family and friends in Christian love.

Enable us to catch a glimpse of what it means to live life to the fullest. Not a life that pleasures itself in the abundance of material things, but one who experiences the joy of righteous living.

May we see in Christ Jesus not only the revelation of your love, but may we also see what we can become if we are willing to dedicate our life and learn to live sacrificially. We live in a time that calls for a people of integrity – those of noble character – and those who offer sterling examples of personhood.

Enable us to build our life around values that endure.

We pray for all sorts of conditions of persons:

- For those who labor under some illness or plagues by uncertainties.
- For those who have lost a loved one.
- For those whose life lacks meaning.

Be to us a presence that guides our steps and empowers our actions to the end that your purpose will be served.

God of Light

O God, whose light does not fade, and whose love does not fail; as we do not seek the sun, but simply open ourselves to its warmth and light – so we do not seek you as much as you have sought us. In your presence, let us feel the warmth of your love, and the rustling of your Spirit.

In the light of Christs' life, enable us to be honest about our own spiritual condition. Cure us, O God, of our spiritual dilemmas. Left to ourselves, we are at the mercy of our own passions and fears.

We seek to hide behind our many facades. Forgive us:

- For hearing your word and not following it.
- For knowing your word and not loving it.
- For believing your word and not living it.

If there is no spark or flame in our life, O God, our motivation is questionable, and our enthusiasm is misdirected.

By your mercy may our pretenses be swept away, and by your grace may our doubts be lifted, and our devotion increased.

In the light of Christs' life, let us catch a glimpse of our possibilities. Let us be that church that sets on a hill, radiating its light in all directions, drawing others to its ministry.

Take us out of the stands and onto the playing field, where the greatest of all battles is being fought, a battle for the hearts, minds and loyalties of your creation. May we be true to the Gospel and bold in our witness.

In Jesus name we pray.

(Also available on audio- "Prayers for Daily Living"- Track 26)

Re-Order Our Lives

Eternal God, who holds the planets in their orbit, yet who understands the desires of every human heart, we acknowledge that you watch over us as a mother watches over her children. Your wisdom is beyond our comprehension, yet we experience the depth of your personal love.

We confess, O God:

- We have followed, too much, the devices and desires of our own heart.
- We have worshipped at the feet of our cultural gods, rather than living by the standard given to us in Christ Jesus.
- We have looked to the world for answers to our critical questions, bypassing your divine wisdom.
- We have molded your church into a secular institution, rather than allowing you to shape us into a divine community.
- We have designed our own laws and teachings that are inconsistent with your Gospel message.
- We have built our houses upon the sand, rather than upon the Rock of Our Salvation.

Grant to us the courage to be honest, to lay bare our souls before you, so that we may experience your gracious forgiveness.

We ask, O God, that you would enable us to re-order our lives by the standards of your choosing. May we shore up our foundations around spiritual and eternal values. May we, once again, accept the disciplines of our covenantal relationships.

Grant to us, O God:

- A purity of heart;
- An humility of spirit;

- An integrity of life;
- And charity for all that is yours.

Draw close to each of us who have special requests. May the power of your presence wipe out all that is wrong, and restore us to our rightful place as children who are obedient to the way of the cross.

(Also available on audio- "Prayers for Daily Living"- Track 15)

Teach Us, O God

Eternal and ever present God, who watches over us with a sleepless vigil; how comforting it is to know that you are our cloud by day and our pillar of fire at night.

As parents enjoy their children, how good it is that you desire and enjoy our company. Your desire is to be close to us, even though we often feel uncomfortable when you are too close.

It is natural for us to turn to you when things go wrong, yet how easily we forget your name when everything is going well. When illness, disease or disappointment occur, your name is the first on our lips. Yet when we are tasting material success, how easily we become self-satisfied and independent.

We confess, O God, that, at times, it takes some form of tragedy to get our attention.

- Sometimes it takes an illness to remind ourselves how wondrous it is to wake up healthy.
- Sometimes it takes separation for us to fully appreciate your life-sustaining relationships.
- Sometimes it takes a state of depression, to realize what it means to be emotionally stable.

Teach us, O God, that you are with us every moment, in the routine as well as the exceptional. Teach us that we cannot live pure secular lives once we have surrendered ourselves to your holy covenant. Bless all of the unions that we have entered into, whether familial or friendship. Strengthen and sustain our bonds of love, between ourselves and you, as well as all your creation.

Speak to Us, O God!

Eternal and everlasting God, Lord of all worlds, Creator of our lives. We gather this day to worship you from the depth of our being. We acknowledge your greatness, and marvel at your goodness.

We ask, O God, that you would speak to us in ways that we can comprehend, as your Spirit witnesses to our spirit. Startle us out of our complacency and summon us to ideals forgotten.

Speak to us through ambitions! Shame us from motives of greed and selfish acquisition. Enable us to set our hearts on things above and beyond us, where Christ dwells. Help us to dream of nobler accomplishments, and to envision a time when hearts divided may become united.

Speak to us through loyalties! Grant to us a dedicated loyalty to our family, a renewed relationship with our friends, and more sacred ties with all humanity.

Speak to us through our sense of gratitude! Remind us of all those persons who have helped to make our days brighter, our journeys more lovely. Grant us humility in the presence of pure grace.

Speak to us out of your love! Assure each of us that we indeed matter to you. Enable us to so experience your love, in such a way, that the substance of all our relationships will witness to your penetrating and abiding love.

Prayer of the Beatitudes

O God, who spoke and the world began, who continues to speak in a language that is universal, heard by all the people on the earth in their own tongue. You have spoken to us visually and audibly through your Son, Jesus. The sightings and the sayings have been recorded for posterity. As we read or hear these words today, may the Holy Spirit illumine and guide us.

Your Word, O God, is a powerful and life changing word. Let us listen today that we may hear your word and respond in faith.

Jesus said: "Blessed are the pure in heart, for they shall see God." We confess, O God, our hearts are far from pure. We, too often, harbor evil thoughts and mask our more sinister actions. As your Spirit mingles with our spirit, may we undergo a refining process that sheds the old self and becomes clothed with the new. Enable us to worship you in spirit and in truth. May we be able to develop a devotional life that keeps us in your presence; a life that shares your sacred thoughts. Increase our passion for clear minds and pure hearts.

Jesus said: "Blessed are those who mourn, for they shall be comforted." Many of us are grieving our losses of family, friends, property or opportunity. You have created us to mourn when someone or something has been taken away. May your divine presence in our life fill whatever void we feel and may our mourning be turned to rejoicing.

Jesus said: "Blessed are the peacemakers, for they shall be called the children of God." We are anxious, O God, about the conditions of our world. Countries are snarling at each other, threatening to annihilate each other. Even within our own borders there is no peace. Make all of us ambassadors of peace.

May the word we hear, be the word we need so that our lives will be purified, comforted, and challenged to become your channels for peace.

Prayer for Parents and Children

Eternal God, who fashioned the world by your own design and who loves your creation without limits, we worship your holy name.

We pause to acknowledge that we are beautifully and wonderfully made, and that your estimate of us is that we are little less than God. From the dust of the ground you made us. You have given us dominion over all living things. You have made us co-creators with you; through that love we choose our mate, and in that love we bear and rear our children.

We realize, O God, being a parent is a mirror image of how you create and nurture your children. You have placed ultimate significance upon establishing a home, and parenting children.

May we as parents measure up to your expectations, and may our love always point to your higher love. May our children honor their parents, and may they be respectful of your divine will for them. Our love, our caring, our goodness, and our generosity simply reflect your divine attributes.

We acknowledge, O God, that all the people of the world are your children, and that you care for us individually.

- Be especially with those who have experienced the loss of a family member or friend. May your comfort make all pain bearable.
- Be with those who face dangerous temptations. Give us the strength and courage to rise above them.
- Be with those who labor with difficult decisions. Enable all of us to see the right way to go, and the power to walk in that way.

May We Reflect God's Light

O God, whose nature is shrouded in mystery, yet whose glory is revealed in the structures of the universe, and whose character is expressed in Jesus of Nazareth,

As the moon has no light of its own, but simply reflects the light of the sun, our lives reflect the many gods we are tempted to worship. No matter what we say with our lips, our behavior reflects who or what we follow.

Teach us, O God:

- To worship money is to become greedy.
- To live for praise is to worship adulation.
- To worship success is to frown upon failure.
- To be content with an affluent life-style is to ignore poverty.

Enable us, O God, to be in the right position to reflect your light, knowing that we cannot do so in isolation from your presence.

- May you consistently find us in worship. We gather weekly, not for a casual chat with a lenient deity, but to be confronted by the Almighty God, who calls us out of this world into a special relationship and service.
- May you find us diligent in our studies, becoming enlightened in our knowledge of your word and will.
- May you find us devoted to Christian fellowship. Enable us to choose our friends wisely, those who are on the journey of faith with us, so that we may challenge, strengthen and encourage each other.

Comfort the Lonely

God of the proud and Lord of the lonely, we realize that pride is our downfall and loneliness is our fear. Keep us from self-deception, from ever thinking that we are better than we really are. Give us insight into the nature and depth of our sin, and through your gracious love, forgive us.

And who among us, O God, has not felt the need for companionship?

- Remember those this day who need the warmth of the human touch, and the caring presence of a friend.
- Remember those who wait by their phone, but no call ever comes.
- Remember those who wait for the postman, but receives no mail.
- Remember those who long for a personal visit, but wait in a disturbing quietness.
- Remember those who need a hug, with no strong arms to embrace them.
- Remember those who would be nourished by a warm meal, but the doorbell never rings.

O God, make us ambassadors of your love! Make care-givers of us all. Remind us that no training is needed for us to be kind, caring and generous, it only requires an act of the human will.

Enable us, O God, to locate those in our church family and community who long for what we can give them, and give us the will to be your people in action.

Bless all this day who have special requests. May all of our problems find divine solutions, and may our needs be met with your gracious love.

May We Admire and Be Formed by You, O God

O God, we bring our restless and disconnected lives before your throne of grace and peace. Our Lord Jesus said: "Do not be anxious", yet anxiety rules our troubled hearts.

We confess that life's pressures and distractions often keep us from our worship, and from knowing you more fully.

- Full calendars, packed days and endless demands occupy our present and threaten our future.
- Work, school or family, perhaps all of them, compete for our minutes and our loyalty.
- We spend too much time comparing ourselves with others, and not enough time looking to our own spiritual needs.
- We often worry more about our appearance, than we do our behavior.
- We are confronted with too many options, and the multitude of choices overwhelms us.

May we listen for your voice as it whispers to our heart. Let us look to Scripture, and to the saints of our faith, for appropriate wisdom, guidance and strength.

We realize that we are formed by what and by whom we admire and worship. May there be no rivals to your dominance.

Worship is such a brief respite for our lives to be impacted and changed. Go beyond our Sabbath encounter, take up residence in our heart, so that your constant presence will be that catalyst that transforms and motivates us to serve your singular purpose.

The God of Stewardship

Eternal God, whose light penetrates the darkness in which we try to hide; whose generosity exceeds the boundaries of our imagination; we offer our highest praise and heart-felt gratitude.

Help us to experience life as a constant exchange of receiving and giving, and to know that spirituality involves us in this sacred cycle. Teach us that we should not give in order to receive, rather we should give because we have already received. Enable us to know that our life is not defined by what we are able to accumulate, but by what we are willing to give.

We ask, O God, that you patiently encourage our stewardship. Help us to maintain a quality of life that is rich in relationships, and less dependent upon material resources.

You have called us to high moments of commitment – may this be one of those moments.

As members of your body, and servants of your kingdom, grant to us:

- Christ-like values.
- High regard for each other.
- Compassion for those who are saddened by loss.
- Encouragement for those who feel defeated.
- Friendship to the lonely and isolated.
- Help-mates to those who are experiencing difficult situations.

Let the desire of our hearts be, to worship and serve your holy name.

Love the Lord

O God, whose light never fades and whose love never fails, we worship you in the spirit of holiness.
How do we love you Lord? Let us count the ways.
We love you with our minds.

- You have given us the capacity to think holy thoughts, and holy thoughts lead us to holy ways.
- You have given us a quest for knowledge, and when knowledge becomes wisdom, it is through divine revelation.
- When our minds are enlightened, we are somehow able to perceive the invisible that is hidden within the visible, and the spiritual that is somehow contained in the physical.
- There is no knowledge beyond your awareness, and when knowledge becomes discernment, we can say with St. Paul, "I know in whom I believe!"

We love you, O God, with our heart.

- Our heart confirms what our minds experience.
- Quicken our conscience through the interactions of our spirits, so that what we feel will be consistent with what we know.

We love you, O God, with our feet, as we strive to walk the Via Dolorosa – the road less traveled.

- Shed light upon our path.
- Direct our steps that we may always be found walking toward you, following in the footsteps of our Lord and Christ.

We love you, O God, with our hands.

- May you always find us clutching the spiritual treasures you have placed before us.
- May our hands always be engaged in the work you have called us to do.

As your people of faith, O God, we share our common joys and burdens.

- When one of us has a cause to celebrate, may it become a family celebration.
- When one of us hurts, may each of us feel the pain.
- When one of us dies, may each one of us feel the loss, and subsequently the sorrow.

Remind us of our holy covenant that requires of us humble worship and obedient service.

Guide Our Steps and Influence Our Thoughts

Eternal God, who reigns supremely over a universe too large for us to comprehend, whose character is without blemish, and whose love is beyond our imagination. We affirm that we experience a personal relationship with One who guides our steps and influences our thoughts.

Remind us this day, O God, of all the goodness that surrounds us.

- We marvel at the beauty of your creation.
- We are grateful for this facility that accommodates our gathering.
- We glory in our church family who cares about us, and who prays for our essential needs.
- We acknowledge your gifts of grace for those who gather in this place, and for your everlasting love that sustains us in our daily walk.

May gratitude be the core of our attitude.

Where we have strayed from your covenant, re-center our lives around the faith.

- May those of us who come to this place reluctantly leave here with job abundant.
- May those of us who come here with weak convictions, leave here with the power to overcome whatever obstacles we face.
- May those of us who threaten to give up, find new hope for tomorrow's living.

Center our thoughts not around our own accomplishments, but upon what you have done for us, and continue to do for us. We acknowledge that we are a people most fortunate, to be part of a fellowship that draws its wisdom and power from your hands.

We pray this day for all sorts and conditions of persons.

- For all of us who have experienced loss, grant us your divine solace.
- For those of us who suffer some malady of body or spirit, may we experience your divine healing and comfort.

May our every need be matched by the outpouring of your divine grace.

God of the Eternal Now

Eternal God, there are times that you seem so close to us, yet, at other times, so far away. Help us to know that there is never a time you withdraw yourself from us.

The absence we often feel is not because you have retreated to some obscure place in the universe, but because, for whatever reason, we have tended to isolate ourselves from you.

We confess, O God, your nearness often makes us uncomfortable, and like Adam, we try to hide ourselves from your constant scrutiny. Even so, your absence deprives us of the wisdom and power to address our manifold needs.

We confess also that life is far too difficult for us to attempt to rely upon an absentee God. We need someone close; someone accessible; someone who cares. Your promise to us is an affirmation of your nearness and constant vigilance.

As we gather in this holy place, we know that your presence fills this room. As God of eternity, we know that you are also God of the moment. As God of the eternal now, we ask that you will:

- Enrich us in our worship.
- Inform us through our studies.
- Encourage us through our friendships.
- Heal us from whatever malady that affects us.
- Comfort us in our sorrow.
- Strengthen us in our weakness.
- Empower us to resist temptation.
- And give us bread for our daily journey.

O God, Be Our Hope for Tomorrow

God of all history, we acknowledge that you are actively seeking to bring about your will for all creation.

Our ancient fathers told stories to their children of your marvelous works. These stories have been remembered for 4000 years. Your Holy Word has become, for us, a book of memories. The gift of memory, O God, is one of your greatest gifts.

As we gather this day to worship your Holy Name, let us remember!

- When nation is pitted against nation, let us remember that you are the Father of us all.
- Where hatred is evident, let us remember the love with which he died.
- Where conflicts prevail, let us remember his reconciling grace
- When fear seems to control us, let us remember that Jesus said: "Do not be afraid."
- Where transgressions abound, let us remember his forgiving spirit
- Where ugly attitudes are evident, let us remember his gentle spirit
- When words are spoken in anger, let us remember his words of compassion
- When darkness covers the face of the earth, let us remember that he is the light of the world.

Remembering our past, O God, gives us hope for tomorrow.

As you guided and sustained our fore-parents, we are confident that you will guide and sustain us. Whatever the calamity, your grace is sufficient.

Be to us, O God, the cloud by day and the pillar of fire by night that will assure us of your abiding presence.

Heal Us From Spiritual Pride

O God, whose knowledge is complete, and whose love knows no boundaries, we come to your gracious throne to seek your wisdom and to be immersed once again in your love.

Centuries ago the Psalmist prayed: "Search me, O God, and know my heart; test me and know my thoughts, and see if there is any wicked way in me." But now, O God, we pray this prayer with great hesitation. We seek to hide as Adam did, ashamed of the dark thoughts of our soul, all too aware of the evil side of our existence that comes with too much freedom, weighted down with wrong choices.

We realize, O God, that which stands between ourselves and wholeness is an honest confession. Your Word reminds us that, "if we confess our sin, you are faithful and just to forgive us, and you will cleanse us of all unrighteousness. Enable us this day, O God, as we receive the sacrament of your grace, that we will bring all that which has tarnished our lives, and leave them at your gracious altar, that we might leave here with unburdened hearts and spotless minds.

May each of us accept the responsibility to clean our own house, and to keep it clean. We seek to be cured from every malady and healed from our spiritual pride.

Enable us to recognize the holiness of common things. May your love come through us as we touch ordinary situations and elevate them beyond the normal, and may your presence in our lives be sufficient for overcoming difficult circumstances.

We Pray to the God of Freedom

Divine Teacher, impart to us the basic lessons of life. You have created us to be free, yet many of us are held prisoner by our own desires and restrictive rules.

You have created us with awesome possibilities. You have said that we are a little lower than the angels, yet by our own choices, we can fall to the lowest depths.

Freedom, in its highest meaning, is a significant possession, yet we have a way of turning it into something trivial and negative. You have created us in your own image and likeness. We are free to love, yet, in our freedom, we have the capacity to hate, which has the power to not only destroy others, but ourselves as well.

We realize, O God:

- We are free to forgive, which is a noble trait; but we are also free to condemn, which brings with it a judgmental and denigrating attitude.
- We are free to give, which brings joy to our soul; but we are also free to withhold, which turns our generosity into greed.
- We are free to be gracious and hospitable; but we are also free to isolate ourselves and build walls between ourselves and others.
- We are free to worship, which inspires and motivates us to be faithful; but we are also free to ignore all gatherings of the faith community.

Teach us, O God, how to truly exercise our freedom as citizens of the Kingdom of God.

Make the Common Sacred

O God, whose truth unlocks the secrets of the universe, and whose love satisfies the cravings of every human relationship, we bow our hearts before you, whose name is above every name, and whose character is without spot or blemish.

In the presence of your divine holiness and absolute perfection, we acknowledge our willful disobedience. When our darkness is exposed by your light, we are led to confess as did your prophet Isaiah: "Woe is me for I am lost! I am a person of unclean lips, and I dwell among a people of unclean lips, for my eyes have seen the King, the Lord of Hosts."

We stand before your bar, O God, knowing that we are guilty.

- We are guilty of being careless and apathetic.
- We are guilty of being uncaring and unsympathetic.
- We sell our integrity for selfish gain.
- We have loved the institution more than we have your church.
- We have worked as if we were the ones in charge.
- We live in the context of material abundance, yet we wallow in spiritual poverty.

For a people too proud and too undeserving, O God, we ask for your forgiveness. Heal us of our selfish pride and restore us to a rightful relationship with yourself and to all of your creation. You have promised us, O God, that, 'if we confess our sin, you will forgive us and as far as the East is from the West, you will remove our sin from us.' We realize that there is nothing in our power to do this, O God. We are totally dependent upon your gracious action.

To all of us, O God, may the common things become sacred because you have labored over your creation, and you have blessed all things with your presence. May the simple things that are experienced through our senses bring us profound pleasure.

May grace, mercy and peace be experienced as we seek to live as your holy people in a world that you claim and seek to redeem.

A Prayer to the God Who Knows Our Needs

O God, our Father, there are no two of us here with the same need. You know our needs. Bless us in each one of our needs, personally and communally. Especially those who are in the middle of difficult times.

- Those who face some difficult task.
- Those who have some difficult problem to solve.
- Those who have difficult decisions to make.
- Those who are dealing with strong temptations.

Speak a special word to those of us who are:

- Evading some responsibility.
- Shirking some task.
- Putting off some duty.
- Playing with fire.
- Wasting our time.
- Throwing away our opportunity.

Let us never bring shame upon ourselves, or disappointment to those whose love us.

- Speak to those of us, who are successful, that we may be kept from pride and self-conceit.
- Speak to those of us who are too self-confident, that we may not be riding for a fall.
- Speak to those of us who are too sure we are right, and too sure that everyone else is wrong, that we may be kept from intolerance.

May your spirit do its work in our lives, that we may have a clean heart, and a perfect love.

A Prayer to the God of Forgiveness

O God, who knows no sin, yet loves and forgives the sinner; we pause in this hour to acknowledge your mercy and to worship the One who is altogether holy.

The Psalmist reminds us that you have created us in your image, a little lower than the angels, yet our behavior gives way to vices that the angels would not consider.

You have made us earthly rulers over your creation, yet we have failed to take our responsibility seriously.

- We have squandered your resources.
- We have alienated our brothers and sisters.
- We have allowed free enterprise to become a jungle of ruthless competition.

How difficult it is for us to recognize and accept our limitations and shortcomings. We too often see the splinter in our neighbor's eye, while ignoring the log in our own.

The greatest single thing we need, in this moment, O God, is the assurance of total forgiveness. And so we ask, O God, that you would:

- Forgive us for all the wrongs committed.
- Free us from our spiritual blindness and insensitive arrogance.
- Remove from us the guilt with which we are so heavily burdened.

May this experience of your grace enable us and empower us to offer grace to all those with whom we are not in Christian relationship.

Deliver Us From Double-Mindedness

OGod, who dwells in high places, yet one who walks with each of us in our daily journey, we are grateful for your ever-present love and for your grace that never wavers. You do not forget us even though at times we act as if we have forgotten you. When we despise ourselves and others, you still claim us as your children.

Deliver us, O God, from the torment of double-mindedness. We continually seek to serve two masters. While attempting to worship you, we tend to exalt ourselves. In seeking healing and wholeness, O God, we need to rid ourselves of sin, which is accompanied by guilt and shame. We have so much for you to forgive. So hear, O God, our confession:

- Forgive us for the mistakes we have made and will make.
- Forgive us for the promises we have made and not kept.
- Forgive us for the bad habits that we have accumulated over a lifetime.
- Forgive us for speaking harshly when a kind word would have been more acceptable.
- Forgive us for the quick condemnation of others.

Enable us to drop the stones we so quickly hurl towards those we accuse.

Assure us again that, "if we confess our sins, you are faithful and just to forgive us and will cleanse us from all unrighteousness." Teach us, O God, how to live in the freedom of your love.

We pray, O God, for all sorts and conditions of people.

- For those who are ill, who seek the best medical authority possible, let them know that where medical knowledge ends, your knowledge begins.

- We pray for those who are sad for whatever reason. Let them know that if every friend is lost, you can provide them with a companionship beyond anything they can ever imagine.

May our every need be met by your divine wisdom and guidance.

(Also available on audio- "Prayers for Daily Living"- Track 2)

Create In Us a Clean Heart

O God, you have tirelessly listened to our complaints and petitions. We have expected you to respond to our every whim. We have acted as if we are in control. We have projected our humanity on you, rather than affirming the divinity in us.

How great, O God, is your goodness, and how greatly we have offended your righteous nature.

- We are impatient, demanding, that everything revolves around us.
- We have neglected our spiritual responsibilities.
- We have suffered from swollen egos.
- We have failed to reach our human and spiritual potential.

We confess that the false gods we worship promises us much, but delivers too little.

In our holy moments, O God, we pledge our loyalty, while in our unholy moments we wish you would hide your eyes, or turn your back.

In the words of the Psalmist, O God, "create in us a clean heart and renew a right spirit within us."

- Give us the grace to live godly lives.
- Grant us the wisdom to accept truth through whatever form it comes to us.
- Give us the passion to seek justice, and to create an orderly society.

We know, O God, that your Spirit can turn our nothingness into newness; our darkness into light; and our misery into joy.

Bless all those for whom we have responsibility: the infirmed, the bereaved, the incarcerated, the helpless and the forgotten. Heal their many wounds, and lift their fallen spirit.

A Higher Love

O God, to whom every spirit bears witness, we acknowledge your love that comes in so many wonderful and mysterious ways.

We confess, O God, the tragedy of our humanity is that we experience love on different levels. On one level we experience a perverted self-love that overflows its natural boundaries in our selfish pursuit of worldly pleasures. We tend to love ourselves with a non-spiritual love that rewards itself in the acquisition and pleasures of earthly toys.

At the same time, O God, we are seeking love on a deeper level, a love that recognizes the divine within, and desires to be in union with your love; a love that causes our hearts to overflow with goodness and joy.

We confess too, O God, we tend to love you for what you can do for us. Even in our selfish pursuits, your goodness and mercy is experienced in abundance. We realize that you love us on a level far beyond our comprehension, with a love that we do not deserve and rarely appreciate.

When we ask for worldly goods, you reward us with spiritual blessings. We turn to you in the storms of life and feel that your presence quiets the waves and hushes the winds.

Help us, O God, to continually reach higher for that love that is infinitely sweeter and far more rewarding. Enable us, O God, to reach that level of love where your mind becomes our mind; where your will becomes our will; and where the desires of your heart kindles the flames of desires in our hearts.

Enable Us to See the Good

O God, whose likeness is stamped upon every human heart, and one who is willing to share with us your greatness. We affirm that you are the God of all creation, as well as the Lord of our personal life. We gather this day to offer our praise and thanksgiving.

We affirm, O God, the extension of your nature is reflected in the many facets of nature. Earthly things have become, for us, reminders of heavenly realities.

Give us the assurance, O God, that through Christ we can reclaim our heritage. You have created us as human beings, which is both the glory and the tragedy of our existence.

- Let us not deny our humanity, but affirm it.
- Let us not make excuses for our humanity, but seek to fulfill it.
- May we acknowledge our bodies as your sacred temple which houses your Spirit.
- Never let our sub-human tendencies override your God-given capabilities.
- Let us abstain from anything that would defile our bodies.
- Fill our empty spaces with divine energy and purpose.

Enable us, O God, to see your likeness reflected in the faces of those we meet. In those with whom we worship, as well as those we pass on the street. Enable us to see the good in each other. May we be slow to speak unkindly of each other. May we be able to control our base desires, and may we be more loving and reliable.

Help us to become the quality of priesthood that you can build your church upon. May we, indeed, become that new creation.

Help us to remember those who are ill and in pain; those who are in the hospital or nursing home; those who are disabled or paralyzed; those whose minds and nerves are impaired by the strains of living. Give us physical health and spiritual wholeness.

Spiritual Gifts

O God, you are the giver and creator of all things good. Your plan of your kingdom come on earth is wonderful and we are delighted your plan includes us, your children.

Your grace, O God, has come to us in so many ways and in so many places.

- Help us to realize that we praise your name the most is when we offer our individual gifts in the exercising of ministry.
- Help us to discover our own unique giftedness.
- Help us to lay claim to those gifts you have so graciously given us.
- Help us to express each and every gift in the common task that is ours.

Let us never be jealous of the gifts other people bring to ministry, and let us not boast of our own gifts as if they were more important. Enable us to see the significance of all gifts knowing with each gift comes a corresponding responsibility.

Let the harmony of our many gifts provide sweet music to our Father's ears. Be our inward strength that we may be strong for outward responsibilities.

Bless the sick, lonely and bereaved. Set our hearts on things above that we might reflect your love in our many enterprises here on earth.

Walk in Jesus Footsteps

O God, whose love greets us in the rising of the sun, and whose grace remains with us throughout day and nights as our part of the earth changes seasons, remind us that you are the One who orchestrates the changes.

O God, you know the fears and anxieties that have so gripped our nation these past several weeks, and you know the relief your people feel as they try to return to their regular routine. We are grateful for your presence in the midst of tragedy, and we are grateful for your loving spirit as we seek restoration from a violent and unpredictable period of time.

Help each of us to discern honestly our own gifts that we may do those things for you of which we are capable; and may we trust that our co-workers will do those things for which they are gifted as well.

May the teachings of our Lord and Christ dispel the darkness from our minds, and may the life He lived inspire us to holy living. As we walk the pathways of our life, may we follow in the footsteps of the One who pleases you in every way. So we ask:

- Strengthen our limbs when they grow weary.
- Elevate our spirits when they become downcast.
- Lift up those who are depressed in any way.
- Calm those who are anxious.
- Guide those who are confused.
- Console those who are lonely.
- Reconcile those who are estranged.
- Bring joy to all who confess that Jesus Christ is Lord.
- Remind us, O God, just as the sun rises every day, your love for us never fails.

We Pray for Great Spiritual Resources

Eternal God, who guards the universe with love and power, be a refreshing presence to us this day as we seek to understand the depth of your love, and as we receive again your forgiving grace.

You alone, O God, know how we give first class loyalties to second class causes, and how we find ourselves betrayed by those things that have become our obsessions.

Grant us a new vision of the causes we should support and serve:

- Justice in a world that has gone terribly wrong.
- Unselfishness in a time when we are caught up in individual pursuits.
- Peace in a day when violence rules on TV, movies or on the streets.

We come today, O God, praying not for soft and easy answers when things come without struggle and sacrifice, but we pray for great spiritual resources that will enable us to overcome the adversaries of this world. We pray for:

- The power to make right choices.
- For victory over powerful temptations.
- For the strength to withstand corruption.
- For stability in an unstable world.

Be with our church family in strong and comforting ways, when we are confronted with death, illness, in the breakdown of character, or in the many ways we find ourselves weak and helpless.

Send us forth from this place to witness to your love as we have experienced it. Help us to be sensitive to the hurts of others. Make our faith contagious. Help us to make goodness attractive.

Prayers for Everyone on the Journey

Eternal God, Father of all humankind, we acknowledge not only the scope of your family, but also our universal disobedience. Indeed, all of us sin and fall short of your expectations.

We come before you with varying ages, a diversity of beliefs, and our own individual hurts. Be patient with our personal petitions.

- Some of us are older, subject to the problems that come with age. Grant us hope for meaningful relationships, a healthful future, and a peaceful death.
- Some of us are young, needing the wisdom of the more mature, yet not wanting it. Grant to them a willingness to accept parental guidance, and other appropriate authority.
- Some of us are on a spiritual journey seeking a closer relationship with you, while some of us face a dead-end street trapped in our own predicament. Give to all of us a clear direction and a worthy destination.
- Some of us experience the joy of worship, while some of us attend grudgingly and give sparingly. Let this hour come alive to all of us, that we may experience a joyful encounter with the holy, and see the endless possibilities for this divine fellowship.

Meet us, O God, at the point of our need, and through the work of your Spirit, may we be healed, encouraged, and transformed into obedient disciples.

A Prayer of Gratefulness

O God, who dwells in high places, we lift our hearts and voices in praise and thanksgiving. We confess, O God, that our thoughts are not your thoughts, and neither are our ways your ways.

For much of our life we have traveled the low road, the road of self-satisfaction, the path of least resistance. It is only when your Spirit mingles with our spirit, does our earthly fixations entertain heavenly possibilities.

When we are in your presence, O God, you are constantly calling us to elevate our thinking, to purify our hearts, to cleanse ourselves of degrading habits, and to walk the road less traveled. Enable us to abandon all thoughts and ways that are contrary to your holy will.

We are grateful, O God, for all institutions that witness to your divine love. We pray for your church, not a product of human hands, but fellowship created through your divine initiative, and maintained by the power of your Holy Spirit. Help us to know, O God, that our purpose is singular, to spread the gospel of holiness throughout the earth. Encourage our discipleship and empower us to be faithful witnesses.

We are grateful, O God, for every human institution that builds character and promotes goodness. We are grateful for every mature and dedicated leader whose teachings are harmonious with your nature, and whose lives are exemplary. We are grateful for boys and girls whose intuition is to follow the precepts and examples of those who lead them. We pray this day for every sort and condition of persons.

- Bless those who have recently lost a loved one. May the memories of the deceased continue to inspire and encourage us to godly ends.
- Bless those who are ill or undergoing tests of any kind. May a proper diagnosis be found with a remedy to follow.
- Bless all who have troubled hearts. May your hand of comfort make easier days.

Bless Us and Speak to Us, O God

O God, whose habitat is not confined to place or time, but who chooses to live within the human heart as well, we pause in this moment of time to extol your greatness, and to offer our gratitude for grace upon grace.

In this holy hour we offer our statements of confession. May our confessions be genuine, and our assurance heart-felt, so that we may leave this place with clean slates.

We realize, O God, that no two of us come with the exact same needs, so may you hear our petitions.

- Bless all of us who face some task beyond our own ability.
- Bless all of us who have difficult problems to solve.
- Bless all of us who have decisions to make that are beyond our own comprehension.
- Bless all of us who face temptations too difficult to resist.
- Bless all of us whose doubts override our confidence.

Speak to all of us this day:

- Who are successful, that we may be kept from pride and self-conceit.
- Who are too self-confident and riding for a fall.
- Who are so sure that we are right and everyone else is wrong.

We remember before you this day:

- All those whose bodies are frail and diseased.
- All those who lack the material means for survival.
- All those who lack the spiritual resources to cope with life's problems.

Let all of us affirm that it is good to be in your house, and that we go forth to serve with a renewed faith.

May Our Faithfulness Live Up to Your Trust

We thank you, our Father, for all the provisions made for the needs of the bodies and souls of men, for the ordered course of nature and for the miracle of the harvest by which our life is sustained.

Teach us to distribute to all according to their need, what you have intended for their sustenance. We thank you for our physical life, with its strength and gladness, and for the glimpses of the eternal which shines through human joys and woes.

We praise you for the human mind and its power to survey the world in its length and breadth, and for the infinities of thought and truth which carry our imagination beyond our comprehension.

We thank you, too, that the world which exceeds our comprehension is not lost in mystery, but that through seers and saints, and finally Jesus Christ, we have been given light upon the meaning of the mystery which surrounds you. Grant us grace to walk in humility and gratitude before you.

May we be ever thankful for your creation and your granting our dominion over it. May our faithfulness live up to your trust in us.

God's Kingdom of Blessings

O God, your spiritual kingdom lies all around us, enclosing us, embracing us, all together within reach of our inner self waiting for us to recognize it and claim it.

We confess that we are overly attached to the things of this world and too disconnected in matters of the spirit. We're grateful for your generosity and patience even though we've been slow to understand and accept.

- You've offered your kingdom of love, yet we've chosen to live a life where hatred often rules.
- You've given us your kingdom of light, yet we've chosen to live in the shadows.
- You've given us your kingdom of reconciliation, yet we've chosen to separate ourselves from those we do not like.
- You've given us your kingdom of hope, yet we're often disciples of despair.
- You've given us your kingdom of joy, yet we find little to celebrate.
- You've shown us the face of humility, yet we often flaunt our pride in arrogant ways.

Open again to us, O God, the doors of your kingdom that we may dwell in perfect harmony with you and your creation.

Bless all of those in our congregation who suffer any kind of illness. May all of us feel the warmth of your presence and the healing touch of your merciful hands.

(Also available on audio- "Prayers for Daily Living"- Track 16)

Thanksgiving for Diversity and the Church

Father God, who binds all humankind into one family, and who stands above nationality, race and culture. We pause in these moments to offer our praise and thanksgiving.

Enable us, O God, to recognize and accept our kinship with the peoples of the world. Empower us to go beyond our diversities and to claim our unity. Give us an appetite for things new and different and an abiding appreciation for gifts that are possessed and shared by others.

May this day be one of joyful thanksgiving. We're truly grateful, O God, for the power of your word that comes to us through many expressions. For the power of music that stirs many emotions. For the gifts of individuals and groups as they share their inspired witness. We're grateful for the Church and for the strong attachment of its members. We're grateful for worship that stimulates us, for curriculum that challenges us, for fellowship that fulfills our longings for significant companionship.

Make us sensitive, O God, to the needs that are obvious, as well as those which are hidden and secret. Bless those who are experiencing any kind of illness. May you work through the caregivers both professional and lay that they may be cured as well as healed. Bless those who have experienced loss of persons or opportunities that they may find in you that presence that fills, but never fails.

Bless us in our common ministry together. May your Holy Spirit guide and counsel us and may our response match your holy expectations. In the name of Christ we pray.

(Also available on audio- "Prayers for Daily Living"- Track 29)

God of Nature and God of Covenant

O God, whose nature is shrouded in mystery, yet who has expressed his love so simply and explicitly in your son, Jesus Christ. We pause this day to proclaim that even though we see through a glass darkly, your nature is revealed clearly and unmistakably in so many ways.

- Every sunrise declares your love.
- Every drop of rain that falls demonstrates your divine involvement.
- The air that we breathe is an inhalation of your divine goodness and generosity.
- Every blade of grass, every pedal of the flowers grow because you commanded them to do so.

O God, you have offered yourself to us in a covenant relationship. You've said you will be our God if we will be your people.

- It is within this covenant that we live our lives.
- It is within this covenant we marry our soulmate and rear our children.
- It is within this covenant that we find meaningful and lasting relationships.
- It is within this covenant that we show compassion and support for each other.
- It is within this covenant that we're bonded in the name of Christ.

We know, O God, the quality of our life does not lie in what we possess but in the Spirit of the one who possesses us.

- In our poverty we can discover richness.
- In our weakness we can discover strength.
- In the forfeiting of our will we can discover and claim your will.

We acknowledge boldly this day, O God, that we're the Church. We are that body of saints who have chosen to follow you and have dedicated our lives to that end.

- Strengthen our resolve.
- Comfort us in our struggles and anxieties.
- And empower us in our dedication.

(Also available on audio- "Prayers for Daily Living"- Track 4)

God, Come Close to Us to Light the Way

Almighty God, from whom all good things come, we know in our minds you're never far from us, yet in our hearts there is a loneliness that craves your presence. Be to us, in this hour, not only one who is near, but also one who gives us the assurance of your divine concern.

Let us know that when dark hours come, your light will shine to enlighten and guide us. Enable us to see the beauty of your created order and enable us to believe in the virtues of a Christ-like life. Make us grateful for the highest achievements of the human mind and character; for the truth science reveals; for the beauty art creates; and for goodness that reflects the compassion of Christ.

Save us from soft cynicism. Let us not be betrayed for shallow sentimentality. Keep us from a life bent toward selfishness. Save us from crying, "Peace! Peace!" when there is no peace.

May we never assume that our broken covenants can be healed with easy words. You're the one, O God, who meets us in the solitary places of our soul as well as the one who confronts us in public worship. May your still, small voice speak to each of us personally to convict us of our waywardness and grant to us the grace of sincere penitence.

As we come with needs beyond description, may we leave this place with souls that have been forgiven and cleansed.

As we come in weakness, let us go forth in strength. As we acknowledge our doubts, enable us to depart with hope. May those of us who suffer with malady of mind, body or spirit feel the touch of your healing hands. May those of us who have suffered any kind of loss, find our empty spaces filled with your sustaining love.

In the name of Christ.

(Also available on audio- "Prayers for Daily Living"- Track 1)

God is Found in Experiencing Forgiveness

O God, from the fabric of the universe you have woven the tapestry of life. From one generation to another you've been constant in your love and merciful beyond our comprehension. To know you is to experience your goodness. To trust you is to be guided by your wisdom. To be recipients of your grace is to know your generosity and dependability. To confess to you, in earnest, is to experience your forgiveness.

We confess, O God, sin has brought to each of us serious consequences.

- Our bodies have suffered from unhealthy habits.
- Our minds have been stained by unholy origins.
- Our morality is suspect because the standards of our society are far below your requirements.

Help us to know, O God, our greatest need is not from material gain, shallow successes or public acclaim, but to experience your forgiveness, and to be at one with you and each other. May your cleansing action be our experience this hour.

- May we work more diligently for truth and goodness.
- May we strive to always act with decency and honor.
- May we become more aggressive in our battle against evil forces.
- And may your Spirit guide us to spiritual victory.

Create in all of us a caring spirit for each other. Where sickness, death, loneliness or disappoint dwell, may we be the ones who bring healing, comfort and encouragement. Through Christ name we pray.

A Prayer of Restoration of Christian Community

O God, whose wisdom is unquestionable, and whose love encompasses each one of us. We offer a full measure of praise and thanksgiving.

- We confess, O God, we are often creatures who stumble in the dark. We need the light of your presence.
- We confess, O God, our ears have heard your word repeatedly, but our hearts have not received your full message.
- We confess, O God, that we have verbalized our faith regularly as your corporate body, but individually our lives have revealed that word and deed hasn't always matched.

Help us to realize, O God, none of our lives are pure and spotless. The sins of our own doing have soiled our earthly and spiritual garments. Let us seek restitution individually and corporately. It is by your grace that our sins are forgiven. And it is by your grace we are restored to full partnership in ministry.

Enable us, O God, to affirm we are not a people of pointed fingers, but we are a people of humble and contrite hearts seeking restoration for all within your spiritual community. We ask, O God, you make us a center of acute caring when one of us hurts that all of us feel the pain. When one of us needs the ministry of the whole body, our response be swift and encompassing. In all matters, let us look to the affairs of our own heart, critical of no one, but affirming of every one.

Seeking Unity

We lift our voices of affirmation as we recall the words of the Psalmist: "I lift up my eyes to the hills from whence does my help come? My help comes from the Lord, who made heaven and earth."

We confess that in our culture there are so many things that claim our attention. We have a way of fervently chasing after false gods. The secular attraction of wealth, pleasure and prestige seem to promise so much, yet when we have them alone our lives are hollow and unfulfilled.

It is our affirmation that there is no god but the God of Abraham, Isaac, and Jacob. We worship the God of grace revealed in Jesus of Nazareth. There is no intelligence outside of your wisdom, and there is no power outside your mighty hand.

You have no rivals, O God, only false hopes fueled by our own selfishness.

Enable us, O God, to know the truth, to feel your presence, and be energized by your power.

We, as a congregation, have entered into a holy covenant:

- To live and work in the spirit of unity;
- To bring our will into submission with your will.
- And to seek nothing except your love and peace.

May our focus be singular and our intentions pure. Where there is discord among us, replace it with spiritual harmony.

There are strong needs among us, O God. There is illness, loneliness, and disappointment. Whatever our need, we are confident that you will find a way to bring healing, companionship, and hope to our humble petitions.

(Also available on audio- "Prayers for Daily Living"- Track 11)

May We Be Worthy of Dominion

Almighty God, whose creation frames your character, we are awed by your creativity and inspired by your goodness.

We rejoice, O God, with the beauty of your creation. Within your creation are millions of wondrous miracles.

- We are grateful for all living and growing things.
- We are grateful for the variety of plants, both edible and decorative.
- We are grateful for the many flowers, on whose palate the colors were mixed and beautifully displayed.
- Gladly we live in the garden of your creation.

There are times our gratitude is in question. We have robbed the earth of its riches; we have bleached the soil; and we have polluted the waters. Grant to us, O God, the passion to preserve what you have given us for generations yet unborn.

We acknowledge the diversity of your peopled world. In your divine assessment, you have called all of your creatures good. We confess that we have sought to subjugate others. We have relegated to second-class citizenry many of your cherished people. Grant to us, O God, the ability to see all humankind as you see them, worthy of our love and respect.

At creation, O God, you gave us dominion over all things. We have misinterpreted what you meant by stewardship. Rather than becoming caretakers, we have sought to control. You have established a world of order, and we have ushered in chaos.

Restore us, O God, to our created status. Enable us to practice responsible stewardship. Grant us a new regard for the worth of each and every individual. Grant us values that never change, and a faith with rock-like character.

(Also available on audio- "Prayers for Daily Living"- Track 13)

Give Us Faith, Compassion, Patience and Hope

O God, whose voice is clearly heard by the faithful, and whose command is sweet music to our ears—we come this day in praise and thanksgiving—for your Church that was born of the Spirit, and through the centuries, has been sustained and motivated by your Spirit.

We confess, O God, that our lives are shaken and unstable. Our fragile vessels are being tossed about by strong winds and turbulent seas. Become for us a safe harbor where storms do not threaten and where blue skies prevail.

We confess, O God, we vacillate between mounting hope and deepening despair. One moment we are full of faith and the next moment we are full of doubt.

Walk through the corridors of our minds and hearts. Purge away any unworthy thought, and remove the impurities of the heart.

Confession is difficult for us, but when we ask for forgiveness, it comes so easily and quickly—in moments of pure grace.

As your community of wayward children, now forgiven and cleansed, we pray for your presence in our lives, to make our witness bold and true.

- Give us the faith to lift the fallen.
- Give us the compassion that brings comfort to troubled spirits.
- Give us the patience to endure the tedious moments of our existence.
- Give us hope for a future without disappointment.
- And hope for a future when love will be our lonely guiding force.

Be the great physician to all who need your healing and comforting touch.

(Also available on audio- "Prayers for Daily Living"- Track 14)

Help Us Become a Conduit for Your Healing Love

O God, through your seasons of special revelation, we have been awed by your magnificent creation. Many times, over the years, we have completed the cycle of the birth, life and resurrection of our Lord Jesus Christ, who opened the gateway to your eternal kingdom. And we have experienced the power of your Holy Spirit as it has invaded the world.

We know, O God, we did not create ourselves. Neither can we save ourselves or sustain ourselves. We are totally dependent upon your majestic goodness and your tender mercies.

For this present time, O God:

- Save us from our fears and reservations to commit ourselves to your high order.
- Save us from wrong decisions that continually haunt us.
- Save us from the uncertainties that paralyzes and prevents us from making critical decisions.

Guide us in our petitions. We often ask for things that benefit us, but are unworthy of your grace offerings.

Thank you for paying attention to small things. Thank you for valuing the seemingly insignificant. If you care for the lilies of the field and the birds of the air, we know that you care about us.

Enable us to help others without need for praise or reward. Help us to become a conduit through which your healing love can flow to others.

Grant to all of us, O God:

- The gift of understanding by which our minds are enlightened.
- Light enough to walk by through dark days.
- Strength to carry heavy burdens.

- Kindness whereby we acquire a compassionate heart.
- The willingness to undertake courageous deeds.

May our deepest needs be met through your comforting and reconciling presence.

(Also available on audio- "Prayers for Daily Living"- Track 18)

May We Worship and Work in the True Spirit of Jesus Christ

O God, whose truth pervades every discipline, and whose love has universal applications. We pause in this sacred hour to acknowledge your greatness and your infinite compassion.

As we stand before your throne of grace, we are acutely aware of our own limitations, and our self-seeking nature. We ask for your forgiveness when in pride we forget we are your people, chosen, called out, and empowered to demonstrate your healing love.

- We realize we have made promises we have not kept.
- We have been quick to criticize and slow to commend.
- We have too often spoken in haste, when silence would have been better.
- We have, at times, remained silent when the occasion needed a strong witness.
- Far too often we have attempted to live off the faith of others.
- We have been reluctant to receive the guidance and power of the Holy Spirit.

Let us affirm this day that we are a people of faith, grounded in your generous acts; that we are willing to submit ourselves to being constantly renewed; that our lives bear witness to the change that is being wrought in our lives. May we worship and work in the true spirit of Jesus Christ.

Bless all of us who come this day with special requests. May all of our needs be met, and may we leave this place with renewed hearts, and with a fresh resolve to be your people.

(Also available on audio- "Prayers for Daily Living"- Track 17)

A Prayer to the God of Diversity

God of all nations, races, languages and cultures, we pause before your majestic throne, awed by the complexities of the universe and humbled by the magnitude of your grace. O God, we know you're not defined by color, gender or physical image. You're not made in our image, but we are made in your image.

With you there is no favoritism. All persons are precious in your sight. Enable us to see the wider boundaries of your creation, and may we learn to appreciate the diversity among us. Give us a sense of caring for those differing from ourselves. Let us be slow to criticize and quick to accept. May our prejudices melt away and may our understanding be compatible with your grace.

We realize, O God, there are many expressions of your love and sovereignty. May our minds be enlightened and our hearts open and accepting. With all of the diversity, we acknowledge, O God, there is but one option for us, and that's in your love revealed in Christ Jesus our Lord.

Enable us to affirm:

- A God who loves us.
- A Savior who died for us.
- And the ever-present Spirit who challenges us and motivates us toward right decisions.

We are a people, O God, struggling with the limitations of our human frailties. Be to us the voice of calm amid the clatter. Make our temptations less attractive and minister to each of us at the point of our pain. May our maladies be cured and our spirits healed in the loving name of Christ.

(Also available on audio- "Prayers for Daily Living"- Track 19)

Eternal Spirit, Give Us Visions and Dreams

Eternal Spirit, grant us the grace to worship you in spirit and in truth. You have so made us that the glory of our lives is not in the things below us that we master, but in the divine above that masters us.

We are somehow elevated by our admirations, and enriched by our reverence. Grant us honesty in confronting and confessing our sins, sincerity in making restitution, and humility in seeking forgiveness. By your grace may our lives reflect your goodness and glory.

Enlarge our thoughts, expand our minds, and enable us to see beyond the normal limitations of daily life. Grant us a perspective, a larger outlook, that we may catch a glimpse of the world as you see it.

Enlarge our sympathies, that we might feel the hurt and pain of our fellow human beings. May we realize we are indeed one family under your guidance and supervision.

We lay our private and intimate needs upon your altar.

- We bring to you all who suffer loss of any kind. How much we need your restoring power.
- We bring our concerns for those of us who struggle with burdens beyond our capacity to handle. We need your wisdom and comforting presence.
- We bring to you all who tackle responsibilities greater than their ability to handle. We need your guiding Spirit to make sure our tasks are done well.

We ask, O God, you be with our church in a special way. Enable us to dream great dreams, that your vision becomes our vision; your work our work; and your will become our will.

(Also available on audio- "Prayers for Daily Living"- Track 20)

Speak to Us, O God!

Eternal God, high above us, yet so deep within us, we come into your majestic presence just now, to allow your greatness to surround our littleness, and to give us, in this sacred moment, a sense of security and peace.

Our prayer, O God, is not for you to change, but for us to be transformed into your image and likeness. Make us receptive to your presence and sensitive to your guiding Spirit.

Speak to us through conscience! Startle us out of our complacency, and challenge us to ideals forgotten or abandoned.

Speak to us through ambition! Shame us for low motives of greed and selfish acquisitions. Set our hearts on things above, of values not of this world. Enable us to dream great dreams, that we may make our world not only a better place, but truly your kingdom on earth.

Speak to us through loyalties! Make us aware of the sacred responsibility we have for family and friends. Enable us to feel the kinship with those of different races, languages and cultures who may worship you by different names. May our devotion to home, country and world be deepened and sanctified.

Speak to us through our sense of gratitude! Remind us again that our faith requires action, that our prosperity requires generosity, and that whatever we give is simply a response to the gracious outpouring of your love.

Above all, O God, say to each of us that we matter; that we are more than a mass of flesh and bones, with no names and no personalities. Convince us that we are known and loved by you.

In your love my we learn to love each other with a sacrificial spirit. In the name of Christ.

(Also available on audio- "Prayers for Daily Living"- Track 23)

When to Be Silent and When to Speak

O God, whose breath gives life to the world, and whose still small voice can be heard above the conflicting noises of our daily life. We are grateful for the timeless truths of your Holy Word. Your preacher of old reminds us again and again that "there is a time to be silent and there is a time to speak."

Thank you, O God, for the gift of silence. You know that on many occasions we have spoken hastily and often harshly when silence would have been the better choice. When we run the risk of offending someone, nudge us into silence. Teach us, O God, the wisdom of being quiet. When your Spirit absorbs our spirit, help us to realize there is no need for spoken language.

Thank you, O God, for the wisdom and courage to speak when the situation calls for it. We know that dialogue is better than war, and diplomacy is better than violence. We know there are times, O God, that cry out for an audible expression.

- Give us your voice when the gospel needs defending.
- Give us your voice when the dignity of humankind is being threatened.
- Give us your voice when justice and peace are at stake.

When we speak, O God, let our words be spoken with tenderness and love. Teach us when to whisper and when to shout.

We pray this day for all sorts and conditions of persons.

- May those who are ill hear your word of compassion and healing.
- May those whose situations feel hopeless hear your word of encouragement and your assurance of divine aid.

- Speak your forgiving word to all of us as we wait in silence, longing to be free from sin and self-restriction.

We offer this prayer in the name of Christ.

(Also available on audio- "Prayers for Daily Living"- Track 24)

God of Healing and Hope

God of healing and God of hope, we bring our brokenness and our disillusionments before your gracious throne, knowing that it is your nature to heal, and to instill hope in the hearts of your children.

There is so much in all of us, O God, which needs healing.

- Our bodies suffer all kinds of ailments that medicine doesn't seem to cure.
- Our minds are fragmented with too many thoughts that have little merit.
- Our spirits are downcast because so many of our relationships are fruitless – and our own self-image distorts your creation.

We know, O God, we can only be healed by your tender touch. Impart to us:

- Your strength that overcomes our weakness.
- Your light that penetrates our darkness.
- And your wisdom that guides us on to right paths.

We realize, O God, we need more than healing. We need to be hopeful as well.

- Give us hope that reconciliation can come out of estrangement.
- Peace can be found out of quarreling enemies.
- Cures can be found for debilitating diseases.
- Sorrow can be turned into joy.
- Out of death can come new life.

Let us go forth from this place healed from whatever maladies plague us, and with hopeful hearts with which we can face the future. In Christ name.

(Also available on audio- "Prayers for Daily Living"- Track 25)

God of Church and State

O God, whose purposes and whose laws pervade this vast universe; before whose face strong nations have risen and fallen away; enable this nation, O God, to know and accept our rightful place among the world's people; and equip us to serve with strength and gladness.

We confess, O God, the Church has failed to live up to your expectations. It has become a fractured institution bowing to the desires of its constituency and ignoring the mandate of the gospel. Our faith has shallow roots, and our actions betray our spoken affirmations.

As the prophet Isaiah declared: "I am a man of unclean lips, and I dwell among a people of unclean lips." The moral fiber of our country is corrupt. We are careless with our heritage, and cynical about the future. Modern culture has become the yardstick with which we measure ourselves. We have placed our material wants ahead of our spiritual needs.

Be to us, O God, the cloud by day and pillar of fire by night, in order for us to clearly recognize and follow your divine leadership.

Be to us, O God, the judge over Church and state. May the Church be a faithful witness to your saving grace and may our nation reflect the values of a sovereign state under your kingly rule. May the Church, once again, become the conscience of the state.

We pray for the leaders of this nation and those around the world.

- Give to all leaders a fresh faith and a bold courage that challenges the assumptions of a secular society.
- May the law of every land rule with justice and mercy.
- May every action be tempered with the love of Christ.
- May the people of this world be enabled to live in true brotherhood.
- And may the peace of Christ fill every heart.

(Also available on audio- "Prayers for Daily Living"- Track 30)

A Prayer of Confession, Forgiveness and Inner Cleansing

God of eternity and Lord of the present, we gather to worship you not only with our lips, but also with our lives. You have created all things good and you have reigned over the universe from time immemorial, yet you have chosen to walk with us, even in the affairs of our mundane existence.

We confess, O God, we seek to hide from you like Adam did; for we have made so many wrong choices; we feel guilty and are ashamed. Our lives are out of control and we need your steady hand and guiding Spirit. We have repressed our sins so far inside us that we have difficulty recognizing it and accepting it.

- Forgive us for allowing the things that do not matter to matter too much.
- For judging too quickly and speaking too harshly.
- Forgive us for our failures and poor efforts.
- Forgive us for bad habits that continually clutter up our lives.
- Forgive us for thinking our sins are irrelevant.
- Forgive us for walking too close to temptation.

Help us to realize the only thing outside your forgiveness as our own refusal to ask for and accept it. May our honest confession and assurance of forgiveness be a sweet sensation to our humble spirits that cleanses our souls from the stains of our selfish desires and ambitions. And may this time of confession, forgiveness and inner cleansing be but a prelude to a life of full commitment and service.

In Christ's name.

(Also available on audio- "Prayers for Daily Living"- Track 31)

Wholeness is Found Through Confession

The Scripture reminds us:" If you confess with your mouth, 'Jesus is Lord' and believe in your heart that God raised him from the dead, you will be saved."

We come this day confessing Jesus is Lord! Jesus is Lord over the universe; Lord over the Church; and Lord over our personal lives. O Lord, accept our confession with heart and mouth as we assemble this day hoping to bring our lives into harmony with your divine will.

There is so much of the world in all of us that we have all but forgotten to whom we belong. We live our lives, for the most part, separated from you divine will and way. We have become a secular congregation occupying a sacred space. We go through the motions of worship with little effect upon our daily living.

Enable us, O God, to truly confess our waywardness, so that we may be cleansed from the contamination of our society. We know that only as we confess will our sins be removed, making place for your Spirit to refine our weaknesses and strengthen our resolve. Make us vessels fit to be used for the work of your Spirit in transforming the ordinary into the richness of your likeness.

May the confessions we make today become the transforming force which prepares us to become true disciples in your work, instead of broken pottery that cannot contain the essence of what we confess as essential.

Confession is the beginning of our spiritual rehabilitation. Life has little meaning and power until we become serious about the ministry afforded us by the life, death, and resurrection of our Lord. We have played at being the church for ages past. Now let us become the true followers of our Lord, and devote ourselves to a ministry that is pleasing in your sight.

Enable Us to Build Our Life Around Values Which Endure

Father God, whose handiwork reveals the measure of your mind, and whose gift of your Son reveals the depth of your love, we come this day strong in the belief you have done for us far more than we can think or imagine.

We give thanks this day for all persons, great and good, who have strived to remain faithful to the tenets of our belief. Those who sought to be a good neighbor, and who have carefully and lovingly nurtured their family and friends in Christian love.

Enable us, O God, to catch a glimpse of what it means to live life to the fullest. Not a life that pleasures itself in the abundance of material things, but one who experiences the joy of righteous living.

May we see in Christ Jesus, not only the revelation of your love, but may we also see in him what we can become if we are willing to dedicate our life to the max, and learn to live sacrificially.

We live in a time, O God, which calls for a people of integrity, those of noble character, and those who offer sterling examples of personhood. Enable us to build our life around values which endure.

We pray for all sorts of conditions of persons.

- We pray for those who labor under illness, or plagued by uncertainties.
- We pray for those who have lost a loved one and need your comforting presence.
- We pray for those whose life lacks meaning; may the void be filled with a certain direction and an abiding hope.

Be to all of us a presence that guides our steps and empowers our actions to the end that your purpose will be served.

We Lift Our Hearts and Minds to You, O God

Eternal God, who has created us a little less than angels, you have given us the capacity to learn and grow; to climb high mountains in our minds; to soar spiritually above the rest of your creation. No matter how high we climb, you are ever before us, calling us to heights unattained. We lift our hearts and minds to you, O God.

From all manner of self-complacency, from pride in our small accomplishments, and forgetfulness of your high ideal, forgive us for living mediocre lives. We confess we measure our lives by the standards of the crowd. We try to excuse ourselves by appealing to common practice. We are content to live our lives by the rules of our own choosing.

Grant us, O God, not only to see where we are, but also where we should be. Give us an independence of mind that witnesses to our own uniqueness, but give us a spirit that is free, yet disciplined by love to serve your high and holy purposes. Let us live according to our conscience, which has been conditioned by the grace and love of our Lord and Christ.

May we see beyond the walls of our own construction, a social order that is fair and just. Let us not become content as long as poverty and ignorance exists. May the seed which you have sown in our soul, grow into plants which offer shade to every weary traveler; and may the fruit from our trees offer hospitality to all who pass by.

May the need of our hearts this morning be met with your understanding and compassion.

Be to Us a Judge, Guide and Friend

"**D**ear Lord and Father of mankind; forgive our foolish ways; re-clothe us in our rightful mind, in deeper reverence, praise."

O God, we glory in your greatness and we marvel at the depth and magnitude of your love.

Be to us what the souls of persons across the centuries have sought to find in you. Be to us a refuge, a peaceful harbor, a very present help in times of trouble. Throw your greatness around our littleness, and encompass us with your unspeakable love.

Be to us a judge. Not a judge who harshly condemns us, but one who accepts and forgives us. One whose mercy is greater than our waywardness; and one whose justice is tempered with mercy and love.

Be to us a guide. We realize, O God, we cannot direct our own steps. We need your wisdom to lead us out of the wilderness where we have wandered; and we need your plan to make our lives purposeful.

Be to us a friend, not an absentee companion, but one available for each day's most common needs. We need the divine relationship which allows us to feel we truly matter; that our life is worth something, and you will not desert us.

We lift to you our petitions, spoken and unspoken. Feel the beating of our hearts as we seek to live with a divine rhythm which gives balance and meaning to our life. Help us to be true for those who trust us. Help us to be pure for those who care enough to be compassionate. Help us to be disciplined and committed in all our ways.

Nourish and Renew Us

Almighty God, whose rain refreshes the earth and whose plants are nourished by the warm sun and refreshing rain. We turn to you that our own souls will be nourished and renewed.

We confess, O God, that we are a people with mixed emotions:

- One day we are up and the next day we are down.
- In one moment we offer our praise and adoration, and in the next moment we are confused and troubled by what we see and hear.
- One minute we are full of faith – yet in the next we are full of doubt.
- One minute we are overcome with your gracious love – in the next we pour out contempt upon our neighbors.
- We vacillate between hope and deepening despair.
- We want the best for others – yet we become jealous when they get what we do not have.

In the moment of worship, O God, we thank you for loving and accepting us even with our contradictions. Surround our inconsistencies with your nature that never changes. Confront our moody moment with your constant love that becomes our model for living.

We pray for all sorts and conditions of persons.

- When things appear to be hopeless – infuse us with joyful hope.
- When trouble threatens us – let us feel the power of your presence.
- When we pray for family members and friends – grant us the assurance of being heard.
- When illness threatens – be to us a curing and healing presence.

May the deepest longings of our hearts find in you – a presence that offers us peace, understanding and the power to overcome our selfish ways.

Direct Biblical References

SECTION ONE: PRAYERS FOR THE CHRISTIAN CALENDAR
Prayer- Your Word Addresses a Broken World- Isaiah (9:6)
Prayer- A Savior to Lift Us Out of Our Predicament-
Prayer- A Time of Waiting- I Corinthians 13:12
Prayer- Finding Truth Through the Indwelling of Christ- John 14:6
Prayer- A Prayer During Kingdomtide- Matthew 6:10

SECTION TWO: PRAYERS FOR THE CHURCH AND WORLD
Prayer- God and Country- Romans 7:14-16
Prayer- A Funeral Prayer for a Woman- John 14:3
Prayer- A Prayer for Older Adults- Matthew 25:21
Prayer- A Prayer for Those Going to the Holy Land- Psalm 119:105
Prayer- Communion- Imperfection Swallowed Up by Forgiving Love- Psalm 103:12
Prayer- Worship in New Facility- Psalm 118:24

SECTION THREE: GENERAL PRAYERS
Prayer- The Future is in Your Hands- Psalm 103:12
Prayer- Life is Good- John 8:32
Prayer- God, Open Our Senses to Your Will- Matthew 7:7
Prayer- Worshipping God Alone Enables Us- Psalm 121:1
Prayer- Here Am I Lord, Send Me!- Matthew 9:37

Prayer- God, Make Us Aware Of What We Have to Contribute- Psalm 51:3
Prayer- Begin Each Day with a Grateful Heart- Psalm 23:1
Prayer- Prayer of the Beatitudes- Matthew 5:3-12
Prayer- May We Admire and Be Formed by You, O God- Matthew 6:25
Prayer- Love the Lord- 2 Timothy 1:12
Prayer- O God, Be Our Hope for Tomorrow- Luke 12:4
Prayer- Heal Us From Spiritual Pride- Psalm 139:23, 1 John 1:9
Prayer- Make the Common Sacred- Isaiah 6:5
Prayer- Create In Us a Clean Heart- Psalm 51:10
Prayer- Deliver Us From Double-Mindedness- 1 John 1:9
Prayer- Seeking Unity- Psalm 121:1
Prayer- When to Be Silent and When to Speak- Ecclesiastes 3:1-8
Prayer- God of Church and State- Isaiah 6:5
Prayer- Wholeness is Found Through Confession- Romans 10:9

Hymn References

SECTION ONE: PRAYERS FOR THE CHRISTIAN CALENDAR
Prayer: Christmastide- Hymn: *Love Came Down at Christmas*, Christina Rossetti, 1885.
Prayer: Send Down Thy Presence, O God- Hymn: *Send Down Thy Truth*, O God, Edward Rowland Sill, 1868.
Prayer: Pentecost Sunday- Hymn: *God of Love and God of Power*, Gerald H. Kennedy, 1939.

SECTION TWO: PRAYERS FOR THE CHURCH AND WORLD
Prayer: A New Year's Prayer- Hymn: *O God, Our Help in Ages Past*, Isaac Watts, 1719.
Prayer: Consecration of Building- Hymn: *O God, Our Help in Ages Past*, Isaac Watts, 1719.
Prayer: Prayer for the Consecration of a Worship Space- Hymn: *Surely the Presence of the Lord*, Lanny Wolfe, 1977

SECTION THREE: GENERAL PRAYERS
Prayer: Teach Us Values Worthy of This Hour- Hymn: *God of Love and God of Power*, Gerald H. Kennedy, 1939.
Prayer: God of Love and God of Power- Hymn: *God of Love and God of Power*, Gerald H. Kennedy, 1939.

Prayer: Take Control of Our Lives and Of Your World- Hymn: *O God of Every Nation*, William W. Reid, 1958.
Prayer: Be to Us a Judge, Guide and Friend- Hymn: *Dear Lord and Father of Mankind*, John G. Whittier, 1872.